Grand Temptations

Delightful Diversions from the Great Lakes State

RECIPES FROM THE JUNIOR LEAGUE OF GRAND RAPIDS, MICHIGAN

A Family Affair

Putting this book together was a true family affair—the Junior League

family and our own individual families. Husbands watched kids while we

experimented in the kitchen. Mothers went grocery shopping when we ran

out of supplies in the middle of the night. Grandparents scoured attics and

basements for photo props. Children posed for pictures and struggled valiantly

to keep quiet while we negotiated contracts. The Cookbook Committee would

like to extend a heartfelt thanks to our families for their patience and support.

And for every one of them who kept asking, "Is it done yet?"

Yes, it's done.

Grand Temptations

Delightful Diversions from the Great Lakes State

RECIPES FROM THE JUNIOR LEAGUE OF GRAND RAPIDS, MICHIGAN

Grand Temptations

Delightful Diversions from the Great Lakes State

Copyright © 2004
The Junior League of Grand Rapids, MI, Inc.
25 Sheldon Blvd SE
Grand Rapids, MI 49503
616-451-0452
Fax: 616-451-1936
www.juniorleaguegr.com

Book Design: Greg Wagner
Photography: Robert Neumann

This cookbook is a collection of favorite recipes, which are not necessarily original recipes.

Library of Congress Number:
2004101924
ISBN: 0-9634927-1-3

Edited and Manufactured by Favorite Recipes® Press
An imprint of

FRP™

PO Box 305142
Nashville, Tennessee 37230
1-800-358-0560

Art Director: Steve Newman
Project Editor: Tanis Westbrook

Manufactured in the United States of America
First Printing 2004   10,000 copies

The Junior League of Grand Rapids, MI, Inc. (JLGR), is an organization of women committed to meeting community needs by developing leadership among women and promoting volunteerism.

Women's and children's issues are at the forefront of all JLGR efforts ... building a better community that values education, self-worth, and diversity ... achieved through the leadership and effective action of volunteers.

The purpose of JLGR is exclusively charitable. The profits from the sale of *Grand Temptations* are used to support the programs and projects of JLGR.

Consumer advisory: Consuming raw or undercooked meats, poultry, seafood, shellfish, or eggs may increase your risk of foodborne illness.

For more information

on the Junior League

of Grand Rapids,

Michigan, and its

mission, please call

616.451.0452 or visit

www.juniorleaguegr.com

When is a cookbook not a cookbook?

When it's also a travelogue. And a picture book. And a glimpse into the lives of some very special people in a very special place.

When it's the Junior League of Grand Rapids Cookbook.

Every book you purchase will help us improve the lives of young people and their families in Grand Rapids and throughout West Michigan.

We've been volunteering our services on their behalf for more than 75 years now. We give freely of our time. But money is the engine that makes our helping hands more efficient and effective.

So we've become rather adept at raising funds. Historically, some of our most successful fund-raisers have centered on fun, festive community events — from gala art auctions to marathon shopping expos.

Celebrations, if you will.

So that's what we decided this book would be: a celebration of the people and places of West Michigan.

We hope you'll join us as we share our favorite recipes, our secret getaways, and our cherished rituals.

It's an experience you won't soon forget.

Just as we won't forget your contribution to our cause.

Surrender to the allure of West Michigan.

First things first: If you're not familiar with Michigan, hold up your right hand in front of your face, palm facing toward you. You're looking at a pretty good approximation of our fair state. Our home city — Grand Rapids — is about a third of the way up from your wrist, about a half-inch in from the left side of your hand. Everything from your ring finger down can be considered West Michigan — the focus of this book.

We may be biased, but we think West Michigan is one of the finest spots on Earth. It's lavished with a bounty of inland lakes and forests, dotted with cities that run the gamut from hip art colony to bustling metropolis to laid-back resort, and peopled by genuine folk who believe in the value of hard work and kindness to strangers.

Our most important and most distinguishing natural resource has always been the Great Lakes. Lake Michigan is the great contributing factor to the lives and lifestyles of West Michigan. These dazzling blue waters shape our climate, lengthen our growing season, and dominate our recreation.

You'll see the effects of Lake Michigan throughout this book—in the distinctive scenery of the seasons, in the abundance of recipes calling for just-picked produce and fresh fish, and in the smiles on sun-drenched faces.

It's all about women, children, and families.

The Junior League of Grand Rapids, Michigan, Inc., was incorporated in January 1926.

Our Mission Statement today remains the same as it was then: to meet community needs by developing leadership among women and promoting volunteerism. We concentrate our leadership, volunteer, and financial resources on supporting the healthy development and protecting the related interests of children, youth, and their families.

Our primary objectives are to improve young children's chances for optimal development and to limit the incidence and effects of child abuse and neglect. The organizations we support have ranged from VSA Arts, which enriches the lives of children and adults with disabilities through art, to West Michigan Gleaners, which collects and distributes food to the hungry. From Habitat for Humanity to Ronald McDonald House, and from Hospice to Mercy Respite Center, we've assisted the Healthy Start Program, Safe Kids, Senior Neighbors, YWCA Domestic Crisis Center, Goodwill, and so many more — nearly 100 different causes over the course of our history.

Table of Contents

Committee Co-Chairs

Natalie Bernecker

Kelly Elliott

Marni Enghauser

Melissa Moore Janes

Kris Wilson

Committee Members

Colleen Lowry Alward

Jenny Barnes

Meredith Beachler

Ann Marie Bell

Chris Bill

Anne Bowman

Jean Brooks

Nicole Canfield

Darlene Crumbaugh

Julie Dykstra

Sara Fink

Janet Goyne

Katherine Klein Gundy

Jill Hilty

Michelle Johnson

Mary Reed Kelly

Virginia Kendrick

Melissa Klunejko

Leigh Kubiak

Pam Liggett

Marcia Love

Peggy Magnesen

Elspeth Minor

Dee Morrison

Joanne Nicola

Shelley Parente

Kristen Ringler

Julie Rupp

Jenell Spindle

Lisbeth Votruba

Joanie Wray

We are grateful for a Bank of support.

Generous financial support for this cookbook came from Mercantile Bank of West Michigan.

Locally chartered, locally operated, and locally focused, Mercantile Bank has always directed much of its philanthropy to causes that parallel our own: kids in need, families in need, neighborhoods in need.

We are grateful to Mercantile Bank—and all of our contributors—for encouragement and support.

Thank You!

And a wealth of creative talent.

We wanted a book that stands out from the crowd. So we went to a creative team that stands head and shoulders above the rest.

Our thanks to the following individuals for their imagination and inspiration:

Greg Wagner and Mike Dykstra of Wagner Design, Inc., for creative direction.
Greg was also responsible for design, food styling, and photo direction. Mike contributed copywriting assistance.

Robert Neumann of Big Event Studios for photography. www.bigeventstudios.com.

Jan Bridgeman of JB Productions for additional food styling.

Appetizers

Above: Herb Marinated Mozzarella (page 19). Opposite page from top to bottom: Cocktail BLTs (page 18), Spicy Creole Shrimp (page 25), El Paso Rolls with Raspberry Chipotle Sauce (page 17).

Beef Wellington Tarts

YIELD: 30 TARTS

Tarts

4	ounces beef tenderloin, trimmed
3	tablespoons olive oil
1	tablespoon red wine vinegar
1/2	teaspoon Dijon mustard
1/2	teaspoon lemon juice
1/2	teaspoon salt
1/8	teaspoon coarsely ground black pepper
	Dash of cayenne pepper
	Pinch of sugar
3	tablespoons butter
3	cups finely chopped mushrooms
1/4	cup minced shallots
	Salt and freshly ground black pepper to taste
2	(15-count) packages frozen miniature phyllo cups, thawed
3	tablespoons butter, melted

Béarnaise Sauce

2	egg yolks
2	tablespoons fresh lemon juice
	Pinch of salt
1/3	cup butter, melted
2	teaspoons finely minced fresh tarragon

For the tarts, cut the beef into 30 bite-size pieces and place in a shallow bowl. Combine the olive oil, vinegar, mustard, lemon juice, salt, 1/8 teaspoon black pepper, cayenne pepper and sugar in a small bowl and whisk until blended. Pour the mixture over the beef. Chill, covered, for 4 hours.

Melt 3 tablespoons butter in a skillet over medium heat. Add the mushrooms and shallots and sauté for 6 to 8 minutes or until the mushrooms are soft and the liquid has evaporated, stirring frequently. Season with salt and pepper to taste. Remove from the heat and let stand until cool.

Preheat the oven to 375 degrees. Drain the beef, discarding the marinade. Arrange the phyllo cups on a baking sheet.

Brush the inside of the cups with 3 tablespoons melted butter. Place 1 piece of beef in each phyllo cup. Top each cup with a heaping teaspoon of the mushroom mixture. You may prepare the tarts until this point and freeze, tightly wrapped, for up to 2 weeks. Remove from the freezer 30 minutes before baking. Bake for 10 minutes. Remove from the oven and arrange on a serving platter.

For the sauce, combine the egg yolks, lemon juice, and salt in a food processor or blender. Add the butter in a fine stream, processing constantly at high speed until thickened. Pour into a bowl and whisk in the tarragon. Drizzle the sauce over the tarts and serve immediately.

Wine and dine.
Tips from Grand
Rapids wine merchant
Martha's Vineyard
located in the historic
Heritage Hill district:
Select wines that
either balance, match,
or counterpoint food
flavors. Consider
your food's weight,
texture, and intensity.
Above all, drink wine
you like with food
you like!

Beef Puffs with Curried Yogurt Sauce

YIELD: 18 PUFFS

Curried Yogurt Sauce

1/2	cup plain yogurt
2	tablespoons mango chutney
1	teaspoon fresh lemon juice
1/2	cup mayonnaise
1/4	cup plain yogurt
2	tablespoons minced red onion
1	tablespoon curry powder
	Salt and freshly ground pepper to taste

Beef Puffs

2	tablespoons vegetable oil
1	small onion, chopped
1	teaspoon minced gingerroot
2	tablespoons curry powder
3/4	pound ground chuck
2	teaspoons soy sauce
2	sheets puff pastry
1	egg, beaten

For the sauce, process 1/2 cup yogurt, the chutney and lemon juice in a blender until smooth. Combine the mixture with the mayonnaise, 1/4 cup yogurt, the red onion, curry powder, salt and pepper in a bowl and whisk until blended. Chill, covered, for 8 hours to 3 days.

For the beef puffs, heat the oil in a large skillet over medium-high heat. Add the onion and sauté for 4 minutes or until translucent. Add the gingerroot and cook for 1 minute, stirring constantly. Stir in the curry powder and ground chuck. Brown the ground chuck, stirring until crumbly; drain. Stir in the soy sauce. Remove from the heat and let stand until cool.

Preheat the oven to 400 degrees. Cut each pastry sheet into 9 squares. Spoon some of the beef mixture onto each square. Fold each square into a triangle to enclose the filling, pressing the edges to seal. Arrange on a baking sheet lined with parchment paper. Brush the tops of the triangles with the egg. Bake for 20 minutes. Remove from the oven and arrange on a serving platter. Serve immediately with the sauce.

Garlic Lime Pork Tenderloin on Sourdough

This is a perfect make-ahead appetizer. The longer the tenderloin marinates, the better the flavor.

YIELD: 12 SERVINGS

Garlic Lime Marinade

6	large garlic cloves, chopped
2	tablespoons grated fresh gingerroot
1/2	cup olive oil
1/3	cup fresh lime juice
2	tablespoons soy sauce
2	teaspoons Dijon mustard
1/2	teaspoon salt
1/2	teaspoon freshly ground black pepper
	Cayenne pepper to taste

Pork Tenderloins

2	(1 1/2-pound) pork tenderloins, trimmed
	Olive oil
1	sourdough baguette

For the marinade, process the garlic, gingerroot, olive oil, lime juice, soy sauce, mustard, salt, black pepper and cayenne pepper in a food processor until smooth.

For the pork, pour the marinade over the pork in a shallow dish. Chill, covered, for 1 to 2 days, turning occasionally. Remove the pork from the refrigerator and let stand at room temperature for 30 minutes. Drain, discarding the marinade.

Place the pork on a grill rack sprayed with nonstick cooking spray over medium-high heat. Grill for 18 to 20 minutes or until cooked through, turning every 5 minutes. Transfer to a cutting board and let stand, loosely covered with foil, until cool. You may prepare to this point 1 day in advance of serving. Chill, covered, until 30 minutes prior to serving.

Scrape the grill surface to remove marinade. Cut the baguette into 1/2-inch slices. Brush both sides of the bread with olive oil. Grill over low heat for 2 to 4 minutes or until lightly toasted, turning once.

To serve, slice the tenderloins crosswise into 2/3-inch slices. Arrange on a serving platter with the baguette slices.

Filled and Grilled Quesadillas

YIELD: 8 QUESADILLAS

The case for Queso.

Mexican cheeses

(aka Quesos) add

distinctive flavorings

to foods. Try soft,

crumbly Queso

Blanco, Queso

Fresco, or Panela

for enchiladas and

garnishes. Queso

Asadero, Oaxaca,

and Chihuaha are

better for melted

dishes and dips—

unlike American

cheeses, they

don't become oily

when heated.

Corn and Cheese Filling

2	ears corn
	Olive oil
2	cups (8 ounces) shredded Chihuahua cheese
2	tablespoons butter, melted
2	small jalapeño chiles, seeded and minced
	Freshly ground pepper

Chicken and Mushroom Filling

2	tablespoons butter
1	garlic clove, minced
2	teaspoons chopped fresh oregano
1½	teaspoons chili powder
6	ounces mushrooms, sliced
1	cup chopped cooked chicken
1/3	cup finely chopped onion
1/4	cup chopped fresh cilantro
1	teaspoon lime juice
2½	cups (10 ounces) shredded Chihuahua cheese
	Kosher salt and freshly ground pepper to taste

Quesadillas

	Olive oil
16	(8-inch) flour tortillas
	Sour cream
	Salsa
	Guacamole

For the corn and cheese filling, brush the corn with olive oil. Grill over medium-high heat for 12 to 15 minutes or until golden brown, turning frequently. Let stand until cool. Cut the corn kernels from the cob into a medium bowl. Add the cheese, butter, chiles and pepper and mix well.

For the chicken and mushroom filling, melt the butter in a large skillet over medium-high heat. Add the garlic, oregano and chili powder and sauté for 1 minute. Add the mushrooms and sauté for 10 minutes or until tender. Remove from the heat. Add the chicken, onion, cilantro and lime juice and mix well. Let stand for 10 minutes. Stir in the cheese. Season with kosher salt and pepper.

For the quesadillas, lightly brush olive oil over 1 side of 8 tortillas. Place the prepared tortillas, oiled side down, on a large work surface. Spread an equal amount of the corn filling on 4 tortillas. Spread an equal amount of the chicken filling on the remaining 4 tortillas. Top with the remaining 8 tortillas, pressing gently. Brush with olive oil. Grill over medium heat for 6 minutes or until golden brown and heated through, turning once. Remove from the grill and let cool slightly. Cut into wedges and garnish with lime slices. Serve with sour cream, salsa and guacamole.

El Paso Rolls with Raspberry Chipotle Sauce

(PICTURED ON PAGE 12)

This hors d'oeuvre will receive raves from your guests. . .the secret is in the sauce!

YIELD: 16 ROLLS

Raspberry Chipotle Sauce

1	cup raspberries
1/4	cup madeira
2	tablespoons sugar
1	to 2 chipotle chiles in adobo sauce

El Paso Rolls

4	(10-inch) flour tortillas
2/3	pound smoked turkey breast, thinly sliced
12	slices bacon, crisp-cooked and crumbled
1 1/2	cups (6 ounces) shredded Havarti cheese
3	scallions, finely chopped
	Leaf lettuce

For the sauce, combine the raspberries, wine, sugar and chiles in a small saucepan. Simmer for 4 to 5 minutes, stirring occasionally. Pour into a food processor or blender and process until smooth. Strain the mixture into a small bowl. Let stand until cool.

For the rolls, brush 1 side of each tortilla with the raspberry sauce. Place an equal amount of the turkey, bacon, cheese and scallions on the prepared tortillas. Roll to enclose the filling. Place the rolls, seam side down, in a large skillet. Cook over medium heat for 4 to 6 minutes or until golden brown, turning frequently. Cut each tortilla crosswise into 4 pieces. Arrange on a bed of lettuce. Serve warm with the remaining sauce for dipping.

Cocktail BLTs

(PICTURED ON PAGE 10)

YIELD: 24 SERVINGS

24	slices sourdough cocktail bread
16	ounces bacon, crisp-cooked and crumbled
2/3	cup chopped sun-dried tomatoes (not oil-packed)
2/3	cup mayonnaise
	Mayonnaise
	Romaine or Boston lettuce leaves, torn into small pieces

Preheat the broiler. Arrange the bread in a single layer on a baking sheet. Broil on both sides until lightly toasted. Remove from the oven and let stand until cool. Combine the bacon, sun-dried tomatoes and 2/3 cup mayonnaise in a bowl and mix well.

Place a small amount of mayonnaise in the center of each slice of bread. Top with a lettuce leaf. Spread a tablespoon of the tomato mixture over each lettuce leaf.

Artichoke Crostini

YIELD: 30 SERVINGS

1	(10-inch) sourdough baguette
3/4	cup mayonnaise
2/3	cup grated Parmesan cheese
2	tablespoons dry sherry
1	(15-ounce) can artichoke hearts, drained and finely chopped
2	tablespoons chopped green chiles (optional)
1	teaspoon garlic powder
1	tablespoon chopped fresh parsley

Preheat the broiler. Cut the baguette on the diagonal into 1/3-inch slices. Arrange on a baking sheet. Broil for 2 to 3 minutes per side or until golden brown. Combine the mayonnaise, Parmesan cheese, sherry, artichoke hearts, chiles and garlic powder in a small bowl and mix well.

Spoon the mixture onto the baguette slices. Broil for 3 to 5 minutes or until golden brown and heated through. Sprinkle with the parsley. Serve warm.

Feta Tomato Bruschetta

YIELD: 6 TO 8 SERVINGS

2	green onions
5	ounces crumbled feta cheese
3	large Roma tomatoes, chopped
3	tablespoons chopped fresh basil, or 1 tablespoon dried basil
1½	teaspoons red wine vinegar
	Salt and freshly ground pepper to taste
1	French baguette
	Olive oil

Chop the bulbs and 1 inch of the tops of the green onions. Combine with the feta cheese, tomatoes, basil, vinegar, salt and pepper in a bowl and mix well. Let stand, covered, for 1 to 2 hours. Preheat the oven to 350 degrees. Cut the baguette on the diagonal into ½-inch slices.

Brush 1 side of each slice with olive oil and arrange on a baking sheet. Bake for 5 to 7 minutes or until lightly toasted, turning once. Remove from the oven and let stand until cool. Serve the baguette slices with the tomato mixture. You may substitute crackers or bagel chips for the baguette slices.

Cooler wine country. Michigan produces more wine grapes than all but seven states. Most are grown within 25 miles of the sheltering waters of Lake Michigan, many on the uniquely beautiful Leelanau peninsula. Michigan wines are "cool climate"—clean, crisp, balanced wines that pair well with a wide variety of foods.

Herb Marinated Mozzarella

(PICTURED ON PAGE 11)

YIELD: 8 TO 10 SERVINGS

5	large plum tomatoes
⅓	cup olive oil
¼	cup balsamic vinegar
1	tablespoon kosher salt
2	small garlic cloves
2	tablespoons fresh basil
1	tablespoon fresh oregano
1½	teaspoons red pepper flakes
¼	tablespoon cracked black peppercorns
2	pounds fresh mozzarella, cut into ¼-inch slices
	Thin baguette slices, toasted and cooled

Slice the tomatoes crosswise into ¼-inch slices. Arrange the tomato slices in a single layer in a shallow dish. Combine the olive oil, vinegar, kosher salt, garlic, basil, oregano, red pepper and black pepper in a food processor or blender and pulse until the herbs are finely chopped and the mixture is blended. Pour the mixture over the tomato slices. Chill, covered, for several hours, turning occasionally.

Remove the tomatoes from the dish, reserving the marinade. Arrange the tomato slices alternately with the mozzarella slices on a serving platter. Drizzle lightly with the reserved marinade. Garnish with basil leaves. Serve with baguette slices. You may also layer a baguette slice, tomato slice and mozzarella slice if preferred. Drizzle with the reserved marinade and garnish with basil leaves.

Nut-Crusted Brie with Jalapeño Sauce

YIELD: 8 SERVINGS

Jalapeño Sauce

½	large red bell pepper
6	jalapeño chiles
¾	cup apple cider vinegar
	Dash of salt
2	cups sugar
1	tablespoon liquid pectin
2	small jalapeño chiles, seeded and finely chopped

Brie Slices

1	(8-ounce) Brie round with rind
⅓	cup almonds
⅓	cup pecans
⅓	cup walnuts
2	tablespoons sesame seeds
1	teaspoon poppy seeds
½	teaspoon salt
	Dash of cayenne pepper
2	eggs
¼	cup half-and-half
1	tablespoon flour
1	French baguette, cut into ½-inch slices
1	pear, peeled and sliced

For the sauce, process the bell pepper and 6 chiles in a food processor or blender until finely chopped. Transfer the mixture to a large saucepan and stir in the cider vinegar. Bring to a boil. Reduce the heat and simmer for 15 minutes, stirring occasionally. Strain the mixture through a fine mesh strainer and discard the pulp. Combine the mixture with the salt and sugar in a saucepan over medium-high heat. Bring the mixture to a rolling boil and boil for 1 minute, stirring constantly. Stir in the pectin and remove from the heat. Skim the crystallized sugar from the surface of the mixture and discard. Stir in 2 chopped chiles. Pour into a small bowl and let stand until cool. Chill, covered tightly with plastic wrap, for 1 to 10 hours. Let the sauce come to room temperature before serving.

For the Brie, cut the Brie into 8 wedges and freeze for 30 minutes. Process the almonds, pecans, walnuts, sesame seeds, poppy seeds, salt and cayenne pepper in a food processor until finely chopped. Place in a shallow bowl. Combine the eggs and half-and-half in a shallow bowl and whisk until blended. Sprinkle the cut sides of the cheese wedges lightly with the flour, rubbing it in gently. Dip the prepared cheese wedges in the egg mixture. Coat with the nut mixture, turning and pressing gently. Arrange the prepared cheese wedges on a platter. Chill, covered, for 1 to 8 hours. Preheat the oven to 350 degrees. Spray the cheese wedges generously on all sides with cooking spray. Arrange the cheese wedges on a baking sheet lined with parchment paper. Bake for 10 to 12 minutes or until light brown.

To serve, place a small bowl of the Jalapeño Sauce in the center of a platter. Arrange the cheese wedges, baguette slices and sliced pears around the bowl.

Spinach and Roasted Garlic Calzones

A hearty, meatless appetizer alternative.

YIELD: 8 SERVINGS

Marinara Sauce

2	tablespoons olive oil
1/3	cup minced onion
2	large garlic cloves, thinly sliced
1/4	to 1/2 teaspoon red pepper flakes
1	(15-ounce) can chopped Italian plum tomatoes
1	(8-ounce) can tomato sauce
1	teaspoon basil
1/2	teaspoon oregano
1/2	teaspoon sugar
	Salt and freshly ground black pepper to taste

Calzones

1	tablespoon olive oil
1/2	cup chopped onion
1	(10-ounce) package frozen chopped spinach, thawed and squeezed dry
2	roasted garlic cloves
1	cup (4 ounces) shredded mozzarella cheese
1/2	cup (2 ounces) crumbled feta cheese
1/2	cup (2 ounces) grated fresh Parmesan or asiago cheese
1/4	teaspoon salt
1/4	teaspoon freshly ground pepper
1	egg, slightly beaten
1	(10-ounce) package pizza dough

For the sauce, heat the olive oil in a large heavy skillet over medium heat. Add the onion and sauté for 5 to 7 minutes or until tender. Add the garlic and red pepper and sauté for 2 minutes. Stir in the undrained tomatoes. Simmer, covered, for 15 minutes. Stir in the tomato sauce, basil, oregano and sugar. Simmer, covered, for 15 minutes. Simmer, uncovered, for 5 to 10 minutes or until slightly thickened, stirring occasionally. Season with salt and pepper to taste. Serve warm. You may store in the refrigerator for up to 1 week. Reheat before serving.

For the calzones, heat the olive oil in a skillet over medium-high heat. Add the onion and sauté for 5 to 7 minutes or until translucent. Remove from the heat and let stand until slightly cooled. Combine with the spinach, garlic, cheeses, salt and pepper in a bowl and mix well. Add the egg and mix well.

Preheat the oven to 375 degrees. Roll the dough into an 11-inch square on a lightly floured surface. Cut the dough into 4 triangles. Spoon 1/4 of the spinach mixture onto the center of each triangle. Fold the dough to enclose the filling, pinching the edges to seal. Cut a small slit into the top of each calzone. Arrange the calzones on a parchment-lined baking sheet. Bake for 15 to 17 minutes or until golden brown. Cut the calzones into wedges and serve hot with the Marinara Sauce.

Two-Tomato Tapas

Flavorful sun-ripened and tangy sun-dried tomatoes blended with fresh herbs. . .a bounty of taste and texture.

YIELD: 12 SERVINGS

2	large plum tomatoes, seeded and chopped
12	sun-dried tomato halves in oil, drained and chopped
1	cup (4 ounces) shredded Italian cheese blend
1/3	cup crumbled Gorgonzola or blue cheese
1/4	cup minced sweet onion
1	tablespoon minced fresh basil
1	teaspoon minced fresh rosemary
1/4	teaspoon garlic powder
24	small baguette slices

Preheat the oven to 350 degrees. Combine the plum tomatoes, sun-dried tomatoes, cheeses, onion, basil, rosemary and garlic powder in a medium bowl and mix well. Arrange the baguette slices on a baking sheet.

Spoon an equal amount of the tomato mixture onto each slice. Bake for 8 to 10 minutes or until the cheese melts. Serve warm.

Chilled Asparagus with Sherried Dipping Sauce

YIELD: 12 SERVINGS

1	cup mayonnaise
2	tablespoons dry sherry
1	tablespoon bottled onion juice
1	tablespoon white wine vinegar
1	teaspoon tarragon vinegar
1 1/2	teaspoons dry mustard
1/4	teaspoon garlic powder
2	teaspoons anchovy paste
1/2	cup chopped fresh parsley
4	tablespoons capers, drained
1	bunch fresh asparagus, trimmed

Combine the mayonnaise, sherry, onion juice, vinegars, dry mustard, garlic powder and anchovy paste in a small bowl and whisk until blended. Stir in the parsley and capers. Chill, covered, for 8 hours.

Cut the asparagus into 6-inch pieces. Combine the asparagus with boiling water to cover in a saucepan. Boil for 1 minute. Plunge the asparagus immediately in ice water to stop the cooking process. Drain and pat dry. Arrange the asparagus on a serving platter. Chill, covered, until ready to serve. Garnish with lemon slices and serve with the dipping sauce.

Hong Kong Chicken Saté

YIELD: 32 PIECES

Saté

1½	pounds boneless skinless chicken breasts
½	cup vegetable oil
½	cup soy sauce
2	tablespoons curry powder
2	tablespoons sugar
2	garlic cloves, minced
32	(7-inch) bamboo skewers

Peanut Sauce

1	cup water
2/3	cup creamy peanut butter
2	garlic cloves, minced
2	tablespoons brown sugar
1½	teaspoons lemon juice
1	tablespoon soy sauce
1½	teaspoons red pepper flakes, or to taste

For the saté, cut the chicken into ½-inch wide strips and place in a shallow dish. Combine the oil, soy sauce, curry powder, sugar and garlic in a small bowl and mix well. Pour over the chicken. Chill, covered, for 2 to 3 hours.

Soak the bamboo skewers in water for 15 minutes. Remove the chicken from the dish and discard the marinade. Thread 1 piece of chicken lengthwise onto each skewer.

Grill the chicken over medium-high heat for 2 to 3 minutes per side or until cooked through. Remove from the heat. Arrange the chicken on a serving platter lined with kale or other ornamental lettuce. You may sauté the chicken in some of the marinade in a nonstick skillet over medium heat until cooked through if preferred.

For the sauce, combine the water, peanut butter and garlic in a small saucepan. Bring to a boil and cook until thickened, stirring constantly. Add the brown sugar, lemon juice, soy sauce and red pepper flakes and mix well. Pour into a serving dish. Serve immediately with the chicken.

Can you say saté?

Saté is an ancient cooking style in which pieces of meat are threaded on wooden skewers, grilled, and served with flavorful, spicy dipping sauces. Modern cuisine has adapted satés only slightly over the years, with contemporary food items like peanut butter and flaked coconut.

Layered Oriental Appetizer

YIELD: 8 TO 10 SERVINGS

Oriental Chicken Mixture

3/4	cup chopped cooked chicken
1/2	cup shredded carrots
1/2	cup chopped unsalted peanuts
3	tablespoons sliced green onions
1	tablespoon chopped fresh parsley
1	garlic clove, minced
2	tablespoons soy sauce
1/4	teaspoon minced gingerroot

Zippy Sweet and Sour Sauce

1/4	cup packed brown sugar
2	teaspoons cornstarch
1	cup water
1/4	cup ketchup
2	tablespoons vinegar
1	tablespoon Worcestershire sauce

Appetizer Base

8	ounces cream cheese, softened
1	tablespoon milk

For the chicken, combine the chicken, carrots, peanuts, green onions, parsley, garlic, soy sauce and gingerroot in a medium bowl and mix well. Chill, covered, for several hours to overnight.

For the sauce, combine the brown sugar and cornstarch in a small saucepan and mix well. Stir in the water, ketchup, vinegar and Worcestershire sauce gradually. Bring to a boil over medium-high heat. Cook for 5 minutes or until thickened, stirring frequently. Remove from the heat and let stand until cool.

For the base, combine the cream cheese and milk in a small bowl and beat until light and fluffy. Spread the mixture over the bottom of a 10-inch serving plate. Spoon the chicken mixture evenly over the cheese layer. Drizzle with 1/4 to 1/2 cup of the sauce. Reserve the remaining sauce for another use. Serve with sesame crackers. You may double the cream cheese and milk for a thicker layer if preferred.

Smoked Turkey Spread with Cranberries

Easy to make, easy to transport, easy to please a crowd. This will become one of your new favorites.

YIELD: ABOUT 2 CUPS

8	ounces cream cheese, softened
1/4	cup mayonnaise
1	cup chopped smoked turkey
1	teaspoon minced green onion
1/2	cup chopped roasted pecans
1/4	cup chopped fresh parsley
1/4	cup dried cranberries
	Kosher salt and freshly ground pepper to taste

Combine the cream cheese and mayonnaise in a medium bowl and mix well. Add the turkey and green onion and mix well. Stir in the pecans, parsley, cranberries, kosher salt and pepper to taste.

Spoon the mixture into a small serving bowl. Chill, covered, until ready to serve. Garnish with parsley sprigs. Serve with table water crackers. May be prepared up to 1 day in advance.

Smoked Whitefish Spread

YIELD: 2 CUPS

2	cups flaked smoked whitefish
4	tablespoons sour cream
2	tablespoons mayonnaise
2	tablespoons cream cheese, softened
1	pinch Old Bay seasoning
1/8	teaspoon hot pepper sauce
1/8	teaspoon Worcestershire sauce
1/8	teaspoon liquid smoke
1/4	teaspoon coarsely ground pepper

Process the whitefish, sour cream, mayonnaise and cream cheese in a food processor until blended. Spoon the mixture into a medium bowl.

Add the Old Bay seasoning, hot pepper sauce, Worcestershire sauce, liquid smoke and pepper and mix well. Serve with crackers.

Perfect cocktail shrimp.

Add 1/4 cup salt to a large stockpot of water, bring to a boil, then add thawed shrimp. The instant the water starts to boil again, remove the shrimp, drain, and rinse with cold water. Cool to room temperature. Put shrimp in large pan and cover with ice. Refrigerate until time to arrange platters.

Honey Smoked Ham Dip

YIELD: 8 SERVINGS

3	green onions
8	ounces cream cheese, softened
6	ounces honey-cured smoked deli ham, finely chopped
1	tablespoon chopped jalapeño chiles, or to taste

Chop the bulbs and 1 inch of the tops of the green onions. Combine with the cream cheese, ham and chiles in a bowl and mix well. Chill, covered, for 1 hour. Serve with wheat crackers.

Easy Spicy Vegetable Dip

YIELD: 8 SERVINGS

2/3	cup mayonnaise
1/2	cup sour cream
1	tablespoon onion flakes
1	tablespoon parsley
1/2	teaspoon dillseeds
1/2	to 1 teaspoon seasoned salt
1	teaspoon Worcestershire sauce
1/2	teaspoon MSG
2	to 6 drops hot pepper sauce, or to taste

Combine the mayonnaise, sour cream, onion flakes, parsley, dillseeds, seasoned salt, Worcestershire sauce, MSG and hot pepper sauce in a bowl and mix well.

Chill, covered, for several hours to several days. Stir before serving. Serve with assorted fresh vegetables.

Adobo Dip

Chipotle chiles in adobo sauce are often found in the international section of supermarkets.

YIELD: ABOUT 2 CUPS

2	to 3 small chipotle chiles in adobo sauce
1	scallion
1	tablespoon chopped fresh cilantro
1	cup mayonnaise
1/2	cup sour cream
1/3	cup shredded Monterey Jack cheese
1/2	cup black beans, drained and rinsed (optional)
1	teaspoon fresh lime juice
1/4	teaspoon salt

Mash the chipotle chiles in a bowl. Chop the bulb and 1 inch of the top of the scallion. Add the scallion, cilantro, mayonnaise, sour cream, cheese, black beans, lime juice and salt to the chiles and mix well.

Chill, covered, for 1 hour to 2 days. Serve with blue corn chips and sliced red, yellow, orange and green bell peppers.

Hip hot pepper. Chipotles are smoked jalapeño peppers. Their unique flavor profile—heat plus smoky overtones—makes them a "must have" in the adventurous cook's pantry. Chipotles are available powdered, pickled, dried whole, or canned in "adobo sauce."

Artichoke Spinach Dip

This recipe is the creation of Executive Chef Jeff Kerr of Blue Water Grill.

YIELD: 10 SERVINGS

2	tablespoons vegetable oil
12	cups (12 ounces) fresh spinach, trimmed
1	(15-ounce) can artichokes, drained and chopped
2/3	cup diced red onion
1 1/3	cups grated Parmesan cheese
5	large garlic cloves, minced
3/4	cup fresh basil chiffonade
12	ounces mascarpone cheese
2	teaspoons kosher salt
1 1/2	teaspoons freshly ground pepper
	Shredded Parmesan cheese

Preheat the oven to 400 degrees. Heat a large skillet over high heat. Add 1 tablespoon of the oil and swirl to coat the bottom of the skillet. Heat the oil to near the smoking point. Add the spinach in batches and sear until wilted, adding the additional 1 tablespoon oil as needed. Remove from the heat and let stand until cool; chop.

Combine the spinach, artichokes, onion, 1 1/3 cups Parmesan cheese, garlic, basil, mascarpone cheese, kosher salt and pepper in a bowl and mix well. Spoon the mixture into a non-reactive baking dish or individual ramekins. Sprinkle lightly with shredded Parmesan cheese. Microwave for 45 seconds. Bake for 20 to 25 minutes or until golden brown. Serve with crackers, bread or tortilla chips.

Hot Cheese Zip Dip

YIELD: 8 SERVINGS

2	cups (8 ounces) shredded sharp Cheddar cheese
1/2	cup finely chopped white onion
2	to 4 dashes hot red pepper sauce
1/2	cup mayonnaise

Preheat the oven to 350 degrees. Combine the cheese, onion and red pepper sauce in a bowl and mix well. Stir in enough of the mayonnaise to bind the ingredients.

Spoon the mixture into a 1-quart baking dish. Bake for 15 to 20 minutes or until the cheese is melted and bubbling around the edge. Serve hot with assorted crackers.

Baked Garlic Cheese Dip

YIELD: 12 SERVINGS

1	large round bread loaf
16	ounces cream cheese, softened
1	cup mayonnaise
2 1/2	cups (10 ounces) shredded cheese blend
1/4	cup minced onion
1	tablespoon dried dill weed
2	teaspoons garlic powder
1	teaspoon seasoned salt
4	cups chopped fresh vegetables

Preheat the oven to 325 degrees. Cut the top from the bread and scoop out the inside to form a bread bowl, reserving the top and center. Tear the reserved bread center into bite-size pieces. Combine the cream cheese, mayonnaise, cheese blend, onion, dill weed, garlic powder and seasoned salt in a bowl and mix well.

Spoon the mixture into the bread bowl and replace the top. Bake, double wrapped in foil, for 1 hour or until heated through. Serve with the reserved bread pieces and vegetables.

Celebrate THIS! West Michigan loves a good party. We'll celebrate almost anyone or anything important to our communities, including asparagus, baby food, blueberries, the blues, cherries, the Coast Guard, gizzards, ice, kites, jazz, mushrooms, pumpkins, red flannel, trout, tulips, winter, and our Celtic, Hispanic, Italian, and Polish heritages.

Salads

Above: Chopped Salad with Dijon Vinaigrette (page 54). Opposite page from top to bottom: Orzo Salad with Snow Peas and Grape Tomatoes (page 48), New Potatoes and Asparagus (page 46), Poppy Lime Melon (page 39), Tuscan Pasta Salad (page 49), Grilled Shrimp and Corn Salad (page 50), Cornucopia Salad with Candied Almonds (page 53).

Bacon Mandarin Salad with Sweet Basil Vinaigrette

YIELD: 12 SERVINGS

1/2	cup olive oil
1/2	cup red wine vinegar
1/4	cup sugar
1	tablespoon chopped fresh basil
1/8	teaspoon red pepper flakes
1	large head red leaf lettuce, torn into bite-size pieces
1	large head romaine lettuce, torn into bite-size pieces
2	(15-ounce) cans mandarin oranges, drained and chilled
1	pound bacon, crisp-cooked and crumbled
4	ounces (1 cup) pine nuts, toasted

Combine the olive oil, vinegar, sugar, basil and red pepper in a small bowl and whisk until blended. Combine the lettuce and mandarin oranges in a large bowl and toss to mix. Drizzle with just enough of the dressing to coat and toss gently.

Sprinkle with the bacon and pine nuts. You may substitute sliced strawberries or orange slices for the mandarin oranges if preferred.

Get fresh.

A general guideline when using fresh herbs in a recipe is to use three times as much as you would use of a dried herb. When substituting, you'll often be more successful substituting fresh herbs for dried herbs, rather than the other way around.

Savory Fruit Salad

YIELD: 6 TO 8 SERVINGS

1/2	cup sugar
2/3	cup vegetable oil
1/4	cup vinegar
1	teaspoon Dijon mustard
1	teaspoon salt
1	to 2 teaspoons poppy seeds
1	head romaine lettuce, torn into bite-size pieces
1	(11-ounce) can mandarin oranges, drained
1	pint strawberries, hulled and sliced
2	green onions, chopped
1/2	cup slivered almonds, toasted

Combine the sugar, oil, vinegar, mustard, salt and poppy seeds in a blender and process until smooth. Combine the lettuce, mandarin oranges, strawberries, green onions and almonds in a large bowl.

Drizzle with just enough of the dressing to coat and toss gently. Store any remaining dressing in the refrigerator for up to a week.

Soups & Sandwiches

Above: Chicken Tortilla Soup (page 63). Opposite page from top to bottom: Steak Salad Sandwich with Fresh Rosemary (page 77), Chicken and Cheddar Chowder (page 61), Grilled Chicken and Pesto Clubs (page 78).

Chicken and Cheddar Chowder

(PICTURED ON PAGE 58)

YIELD: 6 SERVINGS

1	cup chicken stock
1	cup water
2	small unpeeled russet potatoes, finely chopped
1/2	cup finely chopped carrot
1/2	cup finely chopped celery
1/4	cup chopped shallots
1	tablespoon salt
1/2	teaspoon freshly ground pepper
1	cup fresh corn
1/4	cup (1/2 stick) butter
1/4	cup flour
2	cups milk
1	cup (4 ounces) shredded sharp Cheddar cheese
1	cup (4 ounces) shredded white Cheddar cheese
2	boneless skinless chicken breasts, cooked and shredded
2	green onions, thinly sliced
2	slices bacon, crisp-cooked and crumbled
	Shredded cheese

Bring the chicken stock and water to a boil in a stockpot. Add the potatoes, carrot, celery, shallots, salt and pepper and boil, covered, for 10 to 12 minutes, stirring occasionally. Remove from the heat. Stir in the corn and let stand, covered.

Melt the butter in a medium saucepan. Whisk in the flour until of a smooth paste consistency. Add the milk gradually, stirring constantly. Cook over medium-high heat for 5 minutes or until thickened, stirring constantly.

Remove from the heat and add the cheeses, stirring until melted. Add the cheese sauce to the corn mixture. Add the chicken and mix well. Cook over medium heat until very warm. Do not boil. Ladle into soup bowls and top with the green onions, bacon and additional shredded cheese.

Load up your wagon! From beach to football stadium to scenic overlook—tailgating is a time-honored tradition in Michigan. It's evolved since the mid-1800s into a serious food forum for the traveling epicure. Gone are the days of hot dogs and chips. Now it's gourmet salads, sandwiches, soups, pizzas, desserts, and drinks.

Chicken Peanut Soup

YIELD: 8 TO 10 SERVINGS

Chicken and Rice Stock

2	large chicken breasts
10	cups water
1	onion, coarsely chopped
3	ribs celery, coarsely chopped
3	carrots, coarsely chopped
1	tablespoon kosher salt
1	tablespoon whole peppercorns
2/3	cup long grain rice

Peanut Soup

1½	cups finely chopped peeled sweet potatoes
½	cup chopped onion
½	cup finely chopped red bell pepper
2	garlic cloves, minced
1	cup salsa
½	teaspoon cumin
1	(15-ounce) can black beans, drained and rinsed
½	cup creamy peanut butter

For the stock, combine the chicken, water, onion, celery, carrots, kosher salt and peppercorns in a stockpot and bring to a boil. Reduce the heat and simmer, covered, for 2 hours. Remove the chicken and let cool. Shred the chicken, discarding the skin and bones. Strain the stock, discarding the vegetables. Combine the stock and rice in the stockpot and bring to a boil. Reduce the heat and simmer, covered, for 20 minutes. Remove from the heat and add the chicken to the rice stock.

For the soup, sauté the sweet potatoes, onion, bell pepper and garlic for 5 minutes in a large sauté pan sprayed with nonstick cooking spray. Add the salsa, cumin, black beans and stock and mix well. Bring to a boil. Reduce the heat and simmer for 10 minutes. Whisk in the peanut butter. Cook for 2 minutes. You may substitute 2 cups chopped cooked chicken breasts, 2 (16-ounce) cans chicken broth and 2 (15-ounce) cans chicken with rice soup for the chicken and rice stock if preferred.

Chicken Tortilla Soup

(PICTURED ON PAGE 59)

The simplicity of crushed tortilla chips adds wonderful flavor to this soup!

YIELD: 4 TO 6 SERVINGS

3½	cups chicken broth
¾	cup salsa
¾	cup frozen corn
1	(15-ounce) can diced tomatoes with green chiles
1	(8-ounce) can tomato sauce
3	tablespoons chopped fresh parsley
1	teaspoon dried oregano
½	teaspoon cumin
2	(9-ounce) packages frozen precooked southwest-flavored chicken strips, thawed
	Tortilla chips
1	cup (4 ounces) shredded Monterey Jack cheese
	Sour cream

Combine the chicken broth, salsa, corn, undrained tomatoes with green chiles, tomato sauce, parsley, oregano and cumin in a stockpot and bring to a boil over medium-high heat. Reduce the heat and simmer, covered, for 20 minutes, stirring occasionally. Cut the chicken strips into bite-size pieces.

Add the chicken to the soup and mix well. Cook over low heat for 5 to 10 minutes or until heated through. Crush several tortilla chips into each soup bowl. Ladle the soup into the bowls. Top with the cheese and a dollop of sour cream.

Orecchiette with Parmigiano-Reggiano

This flavorful soup is the creation of Josef Huber, C.M.C., Executive Chef, Amway Grand Plaza. Begin preparation one day prior to serving.

YIELD: 6 SERVINGS

Herb Sachet

1	garlic head, halved crosswise
2	sprigs fresh thyme
2	sprigs fresh rosemary
1	bay leaf
1	teaspoon black peppercorns

Orecchiette

¼	pound white beans
1	(2-pound) chicken, cut into pieces
	Salt and freshly ground pepper to taste
2	tablespoons extra-virgin olive oil
1	small carrot, coarsely chopped
1	rib celery, coarsely chopped
1	small onion, coarsely chopped
3	quarts chicken stock
1	quart water
1	pound uncooked orecchiette
2	cups coarsely chopped Swiss chard
	Extra-virgin olive oil
¼	cup (1 ounce) grated fresh Parmigiano-Reggiano cheese
2	tablespoons finely chopped chives

For the sachet, wrap the garlic, thyme, rosemary, bay leaf and peppercorns in a large piece of cheesecloth and tie with kitchen twine.

For the orecchiette, soak the beans in water to cover for 8 hours. Season the chicken with salt and pepper. Heat 2 tablespoons olive oil in a medium skillet over high heat until hot but not smoking. Add the chicken and cook for 4 to 5 minutes or until light brown, turning several times. Add the carrot, celery and onion and cook for 5 to 6 minutes or until the vegetables are light brown, turning frequently. Remove the chicken and vegetables to a stockpot. Deglaze the skillet with ½ cup of the chicken stock, using a wooden spoon to dislodge the browned bits.

Pour the deglazing liquid over the chicken and vegetables. Add the remaining chicken stock and the herb sachet. Bring to a boil over high heat. Reduce the heat to medium-low and simmer, skimming the surface several times. Remove the chicken breasts with a slotted spoon to a bowl after 30 to 40 minutes or when tender. Remove the chicken legs and thighs with a slotted spoon after 1 hour or when the meat is loose on the bone.

Strain the stock, reserving the liquid and vegetables. Skim the surface of the reserved liquid and pour the liquid into the stockpot. Bring to a boil over high heat. Cook for 30 minutes or until the liquid is reduced to 1 quart. Remove the chicken from the bones, discarding the skin and bones. Add the chicken and reserved vegetables to the stock.

Drain the beans. Combine the beans and 1 quart water in a large stockpot. Season with salt and pepper. Bring to a boil over high heat. Reduce the heat and simmer for 75 minutes or until the beans are tender but still hold their shape, stirring occasionally; drain. Add the beans to the chicken mixture and mix well.

Combine the pasta with salted water to cover in a saucepan. Bring to a boil and cook for 8 to 10 minutes or al dente; drain. Stir the pasta into the chicken mixture. Add the Swiss chard and stir until wilted. Ladle into soup bowls. Drizzle with olive oil. Sprinkle with the cheese and chives.

Southwest White Chili with Corn Bread Croutons

YIELD: 4 SERVINGS

Corn Bread Croutons

2	tablespoons butter
1	small garlic clove, minced
2	corn bread muffins, cut into 3/4-inch cubes

Chili

1½	tablespoons extra-virgin olive oil
½	cup chopped onion
3	cups chicken stock
1	(4-ounce) can chopped green chiles
1	large garlic clove, minced
1	teaspoon cumin
½	teaspoon oregano
½	teaspoon cilantro
¼	teaspoon red pepper
1¼	pounds boneless skinless chicken breasts, cooked and shredded
2	(19-ounce) cans cannellini beans
1½	cups (6 ounces) shredded Monterey Jack cheese
2	tablespoons chopped green scallions

For the croutons, preheat the oven to 300 degrees. Melt the butter in a sauté pan over medium heat. Add the garlic and cook for 1 minute. Add the muffin cubes and toss gently to coat. Arrange the muffin cubes on a baking sheet. Bake for 15 minutes or until lightly toasted. Remove from the oven and let stand until cool.

For the chili, heat the olive oil in a large saucepan over medium-high heat. Add the onion and sauté for 4 to 6 minutes or until soft. Stir in the chicken stock, chiles, garlic, cumin, oregano, cilantro and red pepper. Simmer, covered, for 15 minutes. Stir in the chicken and the undrained beans. Simmer, uncovered, for 10 minutes, stirring occasionally. Ladle into soup bowls and sprinkle generously with the croutons, cheese and scallions.

How's the weather? Just look at the WZZM Weatherball. One of West Michigan's most recognizable landmarks, it towers above a Grand Rapids expressway for all to see. It's a great way to monitor weather conditions: Weatherball red, warmer ahead. Weatherball blue, cooler in view. Weatherball green, no change foreseen. Colors blinking bright, rain or snow in sight.

Turkey and Black Bean Soup

YIELD: 8 SERVINGS

2	(15-ounce) cans black beans, rinsed and drained
1	cup chicken broth
2	tablespoons olive oil
2	cups chopped onions
½	cup finely chopped red bell pepper
½	cup finely chopped yellow bell pepper
2	garlic cloves, chopped
2	teaspoons cumin
1	(15-ounce) can diced tomatoes
2	cups chicken broth
1½	cups chopped cooked turkey
1	tablespoon minced seeded jalapeño chile
	Salt and pepper to taste

Purée 2 cups of the black beans and 1 cup chicken broth in a blender. Stir in the remaining black beans. Heat the olive oil in a Dutch oven over medium heat. Add the onions and bell peppers and sauté for 7 minutes or until the onions are golden brown. Add the garlic, cumin, undrained tomatoes and the bean mixture and mix well. Add 2 cups chicken broth gradually, stirring constantly. Bring the mixture to a boil.

Reduce the heat and simmer for 20 minutes or until the vegetables are tender and the soup is slightly thickened, stirring occasionally. You may add additional broth to thin the soup if desired. Add the turkey and chile and cook until heated through. Season with salt and pepper.

Beef and Pork Mole

YIELD: 6 TO 8 SERVINGS

2	pounds beef chuck, cut into 1½-inch cubes
1½	pounds pork loin, cut into 1½-inch cubes
	Flour
3	tablespoons butter
3	tablespoons vegetable oil
2	large onions, chopped
5	garlic cloves, chopped
3	tablespoons chili powder
1	teaspoon salt
½	teaspoon cumin
½	teaspoon oregano
1	cup crushed tomatoes
1	cup white wine
2	cups chicken broth
2	tablespoons sesame seeds
1	ounce unsweetened chocolate

Coat the beef and pork with flour. Heat the butter and oil in a large skillet or Dutch oven over medium-high heat until almost smoking. Add the beef and pork and cook until brown, turning frequently. Remove the meat to a bowl. Reduce the heat to medium. Add the onions and garlic and sauté for 5 to 7 minutes or until golden brown. Return the meat to the skillet and add the chili powder, salt, cumin, oregano, tomatoes, wine and chicken broth and mix well. Bring to a boil over medium-high heat, dislodging the browned bits from the bottom of the skillet.

Reduce the heat and simmer, covered, for 1½ to 2 hours or until the meat is tender. Stir in the sesame seeds and chocolate. Cook, uncovered, for 20 to 30 minutes or until the mixture is slightly thickened, stirring occasionally. Garnish with cilantro. This will keep in the refrigerator for several days. The flavor improves with age.

Venison Gumbo

YIELD: 6 SERVINGS

1/2	cup vegetable oil
4	rounded tablespoons flour
1	pound venison stew meat, cut into 1-inch cubes
1/2	pound andouille, chopped
1	onion, finely chopped
3	garlic cloves, finely chopped
4	ribs celery, finely chopped
1/2	red bell pepper, finely chopped
1	(15-ounce) can diced tomatoes
1	cup sliced okra
1	tablespoon Worcestershire sauce
2	bay leaves
1/2	teaspoon red pepper flakes
1/2	teaspoon filé powder
	Hot cooked rice

Cook the oil and flour in a large cast-iron skillet to form a dark roux, stirring constantly. Remove the skillet from the heat. Sear the venison, working in batches, in a large stockpot over high heat. Add the sausage and cook until the sausage is brown. Remove the meat with a slotted spoon to a bowl. Sauté the onion in the stockpot over medium heat for 10 minutes or until soft and golden brown. Add the garlic, celery and bell pepper. Cook for 10 minutes, stirring frequently.

Add the meat, undrained tomatoes, okra, Worcestershire sauce, bay leaves and red pepper and mix well. Simmer, covered, over low heat for 30 to 60 minutes or until the meat is tender. Stir in the filé powder and 2 to 4 tablespoons roux. Cook over low heat for 20 minutes. Adjust the seasonings. Serve over hot cooked rice. Filé powder is available in specialty stores and some supermarkets.

Shrimp and Lemongrass Soup

Fresh lemongrass provides this broth a light, citrusy flavor. Extra lemongrass stalks can be frozen for up to four months.

YIELD: 6 SERVINGS

1	pound large shrimp with shells
6	(14-ounce) cans chicken broth
1	cup shredded carrot
1/3	cup thinly sliced fresh lemongrass
3	tablespoons finely chopped fresh gingerroot
4	large garlic cloves, minced
1	cup thinly sliced mushrooms
1½	tablespoons finely chopped fresh basil
1	tablespoon finely chopped fresh mint
1½	tablespoons finely chopped fresh cilantro
1	small seranno chile, chopped
¼	cup chopped red bell pepper
1½	teaspoons fresh lime juice

Peel and devein the shrimp, reserving the shells. Cut the shrimp lengthwise into halves. Chill, covered, in the refrigerator. Combine the reserved shrimp shells, chicken broth, carrot, lemongrass, gingerroot and garlic in a stockpot and bring to a boil. Reduce the heat and simmer for 20 minutes, stirring and skimming the surface occasionally. Strain into a large bowl, discarding the solids. Combine the broth with the mushrooms in the stockpot and simmer for 2 minutes.

Remove from the heat and stir in the shrimp, basil, mint, cilantro, chile, bell pepper and lime juice. Let stand, covered, for 2 minutes or until the shrimp are opaque, stirring once. Ladle into soup bowls and garnish with additional basil. You may substitute the grated zest of 1 lemon for the lemongrass if preferred.

The art of food. Every June, downtown Grand Rapids hosts the three-day Festival of the Arts—the largest all-volunteer arts event in the nation. Art appears in many forms: visual, performance, culinary, and more. Food plays a key role, with lots and lots of food booths presented as fund-raisers for area churches and nonprofit organizations.

Villa Taverna Pea Soup

This is a favorite winter lunch soup created by Chef Dino, of Villa Taverna in Rome, the former residence of Ambassador Peter and Joan Secchia.

YIELD: 8 SERVINGS

2	tablespoons butter
1	large onion, chopped
2	ribs celery, chopped
2	large potatoes, peeled and finely chopped
8	cups chicken stock
1	pound fresh peas
1	cup heavy cream
	Salt and freshly ground pepper to taste
	Freshly grated Parmesan cheese

Melt the butter in a heavy stockpot over medium heat. Add the onion, celery and potatoes and cook for 7 to 10 minutes or until brown, stirring frequently. Add the chicken stock gradually, stirring constantly. Bring to a boil. Add the peas and reduce the heat to medium. Cook for 1 hour, stirring occasionally.

Remove the pot from the stove and let stand until slightly cool. Return the pot to the stove and stir in the heavy cream. Cook over low heat until heated through. Do not boil. Season with salt and pepper. Ladle into soup bowls and sprinkle with Parmesan cheese.

Squash Bisque with Sautéed Apples

This recipe was provided by Executive Chef Tim Fairman of the Flat River Grill.

YIELD: 8 SERVINGS

1/4	cup (1/2 stick) butter
3	pounds butternut squash, chopped
2	cups chopped onions
2/3	cup chopped carrot
2/3	cup chopped celery
2	Granny Smith apples, peeled and chopped
4	cups (1 quart) chicken stock
1	cup apple cider
1/3	cup firmly packed brown sugar
1 1/4	teaspoons cinnamon
1/4	teaspoon nutmeg
	Dash of garlic powder
1/8	teaspoon sweet paprika
2	teaspoons kosher salt
1/8	teaspoon white pepper
1	cup heavy cream

Melt the butter in a stockpot over medium heat. Add the squash, onions, carrot, celery and apples and sauté for 5 to 7 minutes or until the onions are translucent. Add the chicken stock, apple cider, brown sugar, cinnamon, nutmeg, garlic powder, paprika, kosher salt and white pepper and mix well. Cook over medium-low heat for 20 to 30 minutes or until the vegetables and apples are tender, stirring occasionally.

Process the soup in batches in a food processor until smooth. Return to the stockpot. Pour in the heavy cream gradually and mix well. Cook just until heated through, stirring frequently. Ladle into soup bowls.

Roasted Vegetable Bisque

A wide variety of vegetables may be used in this hearty soup. . .experiment with your favorites.

YIELD: 6 SERVINGS

4	large plum tomatoes, halved lengthwise
3	carrots, quartered
1	large onion, cut into 1-inch pieces
1	small red bell pepper, quartered
1	zucchini, halved lengthwise
2	ears corn, cut in half crosswise
4	large garlic cloves
6	ounces cremini mushrooms, thickly sliced
3	to 4 tablespoons extra-virgin olive oil
	Kosher salt and freshly ground pepper to taste
8	cups vegetable broth or chicken broth
4	ounces button mushrooms, thinly sliced
3	large fresh thyme sprigs
2	small bay leaves
1	cup pearl barley
	Chopped fresh parsley

Preheat the oven to 400 degrees. Arrange the tomatoes, carrots, onion, bell pepper, zucchini, corn, unpeeled garlic and cremini mushrooms on a large baking sheet sprayed with nonstick cooking spray. Drizzle with olive oil and sprinkle liberally with kosher salt and pepper. Roast for 1 hour or until the vegetables are tender, stirring occasionally. Let cool slightly. Cut the corn from the cobs into a small bowl. Spoon half the vegetables and half the corn into a stockpot. Squeeze the garlic from the skins into the stockpot. Chop the remaining vegetables, combine with the remaining corn and set aside. Pour 1/2 cup of the vegetable broth onto the baking sheet and stir to deglaze the baking sheet, dislodging any browned bits. Pour into the stockpot with the vegetables. Add the remaining broth, button mushrooms, thyme and bay leaves and mix well. Bring to a boil. Reduce the heat and simmer, covered, for 20 minutes or until the vegetables are tender.

Strain the vegetable broth mixture into a large bowl. Reserve the bay leaves. Purée the vegetable broth mixture in batches in a food processor until smooth. Combine the strained broth, reserved bay leaves and barley in the stockpot. Bring to a boil. Reduce the heat to medium-low and simmer, covered, for 40 minutes or until the barley is tender. Stir in the vegetable purée and reserved chopped roasted vegetables. Simmer for 10 minutes or until thickened, stirring occasionally. Season with kosher salt and pepper. Ladle into soup bowls and sprinkle with parsley. You may thin the soup with vegetable broth if too thick.

The great morel hunt. Michiganders are wild for the smoky, earthy, nutty flavor of morel mushrooms, often departing for the hunt at the crack of dawn—just so nobody will follow them! Tip: Look for morels in stands of aspen and ash and under dead elms and spruce stumps.

Chilled Cucumber Soup

This recipe, from the collection of Mrs. Betty Ford, was provided by the Gerald R. Ford Library.

YIELD: 4 SERVINGS

1	cup chicken broth
2½	cups chopped seeded peeled cucumbers
1	teaspoon salt
	Pinch of white pepper
4	drops hot pepper sauce
	Juice of ½ lemon
1	cup sour cream
½	cup chopped seeded peeled cucumber

Process the chicken broth, 2½ cups cucumbers, salt, white pepper, hot pepper sauce and lemon juice in a blender at high speed for 2 minutes. Add the sour cream and process for 2 minutes.

Adjust the seasonings to taste. Chill thoroughly before serving. Ladle into soup bowls and top with ½ cup cucumber.

Got muck?

Celery is grown in dark, moist organic soil called muck. Michigan muck produces more celery than all but one or two other states. A natural health food, celery provides oodles of fiber, folacin, potassium, and vitamin C—but very few calories.

Spanish Blender Gazpacho

YIELD: 12 SERVINGS

1	(46-ounce) can tomato juice
2	cups chopped peeled tomatoes
1	cup finely chopped green bell pepper
1	cup finely chopped celery
1	cup finely chopped seeded cucumber
½	cup finely chopped onion
2	tablespoons red wine vinegar
1	tablespoon vegetable oil
1	tablespoon fresh lemon juice
2	tablespoons chopped fresh parsley
1	teaspoon salt
½	teaspoon pepper
1	teaspoon Worcestershire sauce
	Hot red pepper sauce to taste
	Sour cream
	Avocado slices

Combine the tomato juice, tomatoes, bell pepper, celery and cucumber in a large bowl and mix well. Add the onion, vinegar, oil, lemon juice, parsley, salt, pepper, Worcestershire sauce and red pepper sauce and mix well.

Process in batches for 30 seconds in a blender. The mixture will be chunky. Pour into a large bowl. Chill, covered, for several hours to allow the flavors to blend. Ladle into soup bowls. Serve with a dollop of sour cream and avocado slices if desired.

Steak Salad Sandwiches with Fresh Rosemary

(PICTURED ON PAGE 60)

YIELD: 4 SANDWICHES

1½	pounds grilled sirloin steak
3	tablespoons capers, chopped
2	tablespoons minced red onion
1	tablespoon Dijon mustard
1	tablespoon chopped fresh rosemary
5	tablespoons mayonnaise
	Salt and freshly ground pepper to taste
8	(½-inch-thick) slices crusty bread
	Mayonnaise
8	thin slices tomato
	Leaf lettuce

Cut the steak into ½-inch pieces. Combine with the capers, onion, mustard, rosemary and 5 tablespoons mayonnaise in a bowl and toss to mix well. Season with salt and pepper. Chill, covered, for several hours to allow the flavors to blend.

Spread 1 side of each bread slice with additional mayonnaise. Spread the steak salad on 4 of the bread slices. Top each with 2 slices of the tomato, lettuce and the remaining bread slices. Cut into halves diagonally and serve immediately.

Salade Niçoise Sandwiches

YIELD: 6 SANDWICHES

2	(12-ounce) cans water-packed albacore tuna, drained
4	tablespoons capers
⅓	to ½ cup mayonnaise, or to taste
2	tablespoons fresh lemon juice
¼	to ½ teaspoon freshly ground pepper
1	(2-pound) soft round bread loaf
½	cup finely chopped kalamata olives
2	small bunches arugula or watercress
2	tomatoes, thinly sliced
½	small red onion, thinly sliced

Combine the tuna, capers, mayonnaise and lemon juice in a medium bowl and mix well. Season with the pepper. Cut the bread in half horizontally. Scoop out the inside of each bread half, leaving a ½-inch-thick crust. Mash the olives in a small bowl. Spread the olives over the inside of each bread half.

Layer half of the arugula over the prepared bottom half of the bread. Spread with the tuna mixture and top with the tomatoes, onion and remaining arugula. Replace the top half of the bread. Chill, wrapped in foil, until ready to serve. Cut into 6 wedges and serve.

Grilled Chicken and Pesto Clubs

(PICTURED ON PAGE 58)

YIELD: 4 SANDWICHES

Pesto

1	cup firmly packed fresh basil leaves
1	cup (4 ounces) shredded fresh Parmesan cheese
1/2	cup pine nuts, toasted
1/2	cup olive oil
3	garlic cloves

Club Sandwich

4	(5-ounce) boneless skinless chicken breasts
1/2	teaspoon salt
1/2	teaspoon freshly ground pepper
12	slices whole wheat bread, lightly toasted
3	ounces goat cheese, crumbled
1	large avocado, sliced
4	Roma tomatoes, thinly sliced
8	slices bacon, crisp-cooked and halved
2	cups baby salad greens

For the pesto, process the basil, Parmesan cheese, pine nuts, olive oil and garlic in a food processor or blender until smooth, stopping and scraping the side occasionally. Spoon into a small bowl and chill, covered, for up to 1 week.

For the sandwiches, season the chicken with the salt and pepper. Grill the chicken over hot coals for 8 to 10 minutes on each side or until cooked through. Remove from the heat and let stand for 10 minutes. Cut into 1/2-inch slices.

Spread 1 side of each bread slice lightly with the pesto. Layer the chicken, goat cheese and avocado on 4 of the bread slices. Top with 4 of the bread slices, pesto side up. Layer with the tomatoes, bacon and salad greens. Top with the 4 remaining bread slices, pesto side down. Cut into quarters and serve.

Smoked Turkey Wraps

For special occasions, wraps can be rolled up in colorful paper, cut in half, and tied decoratively with raffia.

YIELD: 8 WRAPS

Caramelized Onions

2	tablespoons olive oil
2	large sweet onions, finely chopped
1	tablespoon sugar
2	teaspoons balsamic vinegar

Turkey Wraps

1	(14-ounce) can artichoke hearts, drained and finely chopped
13	ounces boursin cheese
8	(10-inch) flour tortillas
1½	pounds shaved smoked turkey
16	slices bacon, crisp-cooked and crumbled
4	cups mixed baby salad greens

For the onions, heat the olive oil in a large skillet over medium-high heat. Add the onions and sugar and cook for 20 minutes or until the onions are caramel-colored, stirring frequently. Stir in the vinegar. Remove from the heat and let stand until cool.

For the wraps, combine the artichokes and cheese in a small bowl and mix well. Spread the mixture evenly over 1 side of each tortilla. Layer the caramelized onions, turkey, bacon and salad greens over the prepared tortillas. Roll to enclose the filling and secure with a wooden pick. Cut into halves to serve. You may substitute pita wraps, flatbread or pillow bread for the tortillas if desired.

Grilled Vegetable Sandwiches with Havarti

YIELD: 2 SANDWICHES

1	large garlic head
2	teaspoons olive oil
1	large plum tomato, peeled, seeded and finely chopped
1/4	teaspoon red pepper flakes
1	teaspoon balsamic vinegar
1	teaspoon dried mixed herbs, or 1 tablespoon fresh mixed herbs, such as basil, parsley and oregano
1/4	teaspoon kosher salt
1	teaspoon olive oil
1	small eggplant
	Kosher salt to taste
1	portobello mushroom cap
1/2	red bell pepper, cut in half
1/2	yellow bell pepper, cut in half
2	(6-inch) pieces baguette, sliced in half horizontally
4	slices havarti cheese
	Leaf lettuce
	Freshly ground pepper to taste

Preheat the oven to 400 degrees. Slice 1/2 inch off the top of the garlic head. Pour 2 teaspoons olive oil over the garlic and wrap in foil. Bake for 20 to 30 minutes or until soft. Remove from the oven and let stand for 15 minutes. Squeeze the garlic into a medium bowl and discard the skins. Add the tomato, red pepper, vinegar, herbs, 1/4 teaspoon kosher salt and 1 teaspoon olive oil and mash until of a coarse paste consistency.

Cut the eggplant lengthwise into 1/4-inch slices. Sprinkle with kosher salt to taste and place in a colander. Let stand for 15 to 20 minutes; rinse and pat dry.

Spray the eggplant, mushroom and bell peppers with olive oil cooking spray. Grill over medium heat for 4 to 6 minutes, turning once. Remove the vegetables to a platter. Cut the mushroom into 1/4-inch slices.

Spray the baguette with olive oil cooking spray. Place on the grill, cut side down, and grill for 1 to 2 minutes or until lightly toasted. Spread the garlic mixture over the bottom halves of the baguette pieces. Layer the vegetables, cheese and lettuce over the prepared baguettes. Season with kosher salt and pepper to taste and top with the remaining baguette halves.

Greek Grilled Cheese Sandwiches

YIELD: 4 SANDWICHES

8	slices sourdough bread
1/2	cup (about) olive oil
10	ounces feta cheese
2	large tomatoes, thinly sliced
	Onion, thinly sliced and separated into rings
4	teaspoons finely chopped fresh oregano
	Salt and freshly ground pepper to taste
2	tablespoons chopped kalamata olives (optional)

Brush 1 side of 4 bread slices with some of the olive oil and place, oil side down, on a work surface. Cut the feta cheese into thin slices and place on top of the bread. Top each with 3 to 4 tomato slices and several onion rings. Season with the oregano, salt and pepper. Sprinkle with the olives. Brush 1 side of the remaining bread slices with the remaining olive oil and place, oil side up, on the sandwiches.

Cook the sandwiches in a large nonstick skillet over medium heat for 3 to 4 minutes per side or until golden brown. The cheese will remain firm. Cut into halves and serve.

Tarragon Tea Sandwiches

YIELD: 6 SANDWICHES

8	eggs, hard-cooked and finely chopped
3	tablespoons finely chopped shallots
1 1/2	tablespoons finely chopped fresh tarragon
1 1/2	tablespoons white wine vinegar
1/2	cup mayonnaise
	Kosher salt and freshly ground pepper to taste
12	slices seedless rye bread, crusts removed
3	cups mixed baby salad greens
	Mayonnaise

Combine the eggs, shallots, tarragon, vinegar and 1/2 cup mayonnaise in a bowl and mix well. Season with kosher salt and pepper. You may prepare the mixture to this point and store, covered, in the refrigerator up to 1 day in advance.

Spread the egg mixture evenly onto 6 bread slices. Top with the salad greens. Spread a small amount of mayonnaise on the remaining 6 bread slices and place on the sandwiches. Cut into quarters and serve.

Breads & Brunch

Above: Baked French Toast with Berries (page 96). Opposite page from top to bottom: Cheddar Cheese Popovers (page 91), Banana Streusel Bread (page 85), Spinach and Cheese Strata with Sourdough (page 100), Blueberry Coffee Cake with Coconut Streusel (page 92).

Banana Streusel Bread

(PICTURED ON PAGE 82)

You have never tasted banana bread quite like this!

YIELD: 1 LOAF

Streusel Topping

2/3	cup flour
1/2	cup packed brown sugar
1	teaspoon cinnamon
1/3	cup cold butter, finely chopped

Bread

1/2	cup (1 stick) butter, softened
1	cup sugar
2	eggs
2	cups flour
1	teaspoon baking soda
1/4	teaspoon salt
3/4	cup buttermilk
2	ripe bananas, mashed

For the topping, combine the flour, brown sugar and cinnamon in a small bowl. Cut in the butter until crumbly.

For the bread, preheat the oven to 350 degrees. Cream the butter and sugar in a mixing bowl until light and fluffy. Beat in the eggs. Sift the flour, baking soda and salt into a small bowl.

Add to the creamed mixture alternately with the buttermilk, mixing well after each addition. Add the bananas and mix well. Pour the batter into a well-greased 10-inch loaf pan. Sprinkle with the topping. Bake for 40 to 45 minutes or until the topping begins to brown. Remove to a wire rack to cool completely.

Spotlight:
Grand Rapids
Children's Museum

Learn to play, play
to learn. Since 1997,
the Grand Rapids
Children's Museum
has celebrated
childhood and the
joy of learning. It's
touchy, it's feely, it's
good old-fashioned
hands-on fun! GRCM's
interactive exhibits
and programming
invite children to
experience a new
museum every time
they visit.

Java Spice Bread

A blend of fragrant spices and a cup of brewed coffee provide this bread with a rich, deep color.

YIELD: 2 LOAVES

Who's cookin' in the kitchen?

Years ago, women could not contract, could not purchase property, could not own anything, and could not vote. We've all come a long way since then. Today, men and women have options: to work, to marry, to bear children, to pursue education. The Perry & Stuursma Law Firm salutes the Junior League of Grand Rapids for helping meet our community's needs by developing leadership among women.

Special thanks to Perry & Stuursma, The Family Law Firm of West Michigan

1	cup raisins
3½	cups plus 1 teaspoon flour
1¼	cups packed brown sugar
1	tablespoon baking powder
1	teaspoon baking soda
1	teaspoon salt
2	teaspoons cinnamon
1	teaspoon allspice
1	teaspoon cloves
½	teaspoon nutmeg
4	eggs, slightly beaten
1½	cups honey
¼	cup (½ stick) butter, melted and cooled
1	cup cold strong black coffee
1	cup chopped pecans

Combine the raisins with water to cover in a small microwaveable bowl. Microwave on High for 3 minutes; drain. Remove the raisins to a paper towel and let stand until cool. Place the raisins in a small bowl, sprinkle with 1 teaspoon flour and toss to coat.

Preheat the oven to 350 degrees. Combine 3½ cups flour, the brown sugar, baking powder, baking soda, salt, cinnamon, allspice, cloves and nutmeg in a large bowl.

Combine the eggs, honey, butter and coffee in a bowl and mix well. Add to the dry ingredients and stir just until mixed. Stir in the pecans and raisins. Pour into 2 greased and floured 9-inch loaf pans. Bake for 1 hour. Cool in the pan for 15 minutes. Remove to a wire rack to cool completely. Store, wrapped in plastic wrap, at room temperature for up to 1 week. The loaves also freeze well.

Poppy Seed Bread with Almond Glaze

YIELD: 1 LOAF

Bread

3	cups flour
1½	teaspoons baking powder
½	teaspoon salt
2	cups sugar
3	eggs
1½	cups milk
1	cup vegetable oil
1½	teaspoons vanilla extract
1½	teaspoons almond extract
1½	teaspoons butter flavoring
¼	cup poppy seeds

Almond Glaze

1	cup confectioners' sugar
¼	cup orange juice
1	teaspoon vanilla extract
1	teaspoon almond extract
1	teaspoon butter flavoring

For the bread, preheat the oven to 350 degrees. Combine the flour, baking powder and salt in a large bowl. Combine the sugar, eggs, milk, oil, vanilla, almond extract and butter flavoring in a bowl and whisk until blended. Add to the dry ingredients and stir until smooth. Stir in the poppy seeds. Pour into a greased 9-inch loaf pan. Bake for 90 minutes.

For the glaze, combine the confectioners' sugar, orange juice, vanilla, almond extract and butter flavoring in a small bowl and whisk until smooth. Brush the glaze over the hot bread. Cool in the pan for several minutes. Remove to a wire rack to cool completely.

Whole Wheat Zucchini Bread

This rather unusual loaf has a very pleasant, slightly sweet flavor and a distinctive texture.

YIELD: 2 LOAVES

3	eggs
2	cups sugar
1	cup vegetable oil
2	cups grated peeled zucchini
1	tablespoon vanilla extract
3	cups whole wheat flour
1	teaspoon salt
1	teaspoon baking soda
1/4	teaspoon baking powder
1	tablespoon cinnamon
1	cup coarsely chopped hazelnuts or walnuts

Preheat the oven to 350 degrees. Whisk the eggs in a large bowl until light and foamy. Add the sugar, oil, zucchini and vanilla and mix well. Sift together the flour, salt, baking soda, baking powder and cinnamon. Add to the zucchini mixture and mix well. Stir in the hazelnuts.

Pour into 2 lightly greased 9-inch loaf pans. Bake for 60 minutes. Remove to a wire rack to cool completely. Store, wrapped in plastic wrap, at room temperature for up to 1 week.

Sun-Dried Tomato Bread

YIELD: 1 LOAF

2	garlic cloves
2½	cups flour
2	teaspoons baking powder
1¼	teaspoons salt
½	teaspoon baking soda
1	bunch green onions
⅓	cup oil-pack sun-dried tomatoes
5	ounces provolone cheese, grated
2	teaspoons chopped fresh rosemary
¾	teaspoon black pepper
⅓	cup toasted pine nuts
2	tablespoons shortening
2	tablespoons sugar
2	eggs
1¼	cups buttermilk

Combine the unpeeled garlic with water to cover in a small saucepan. Bring to a boil and cook for 15 minutes; drain. Peel the garlic and place in a small bowl. Mash with a fork and let stand until cool.

Preheat the oven to 350 degrees. Combine the flour, baking powder, salt and baking soda in a large bowl. Slice the bulbs and 1 inch of the tops of the green onions. Drain the tomatoes, reserving 2 tablespoons of the oil. Add the green onions, tomatoes, cheese, rosemary, pepper and pine nuts to the flour mixture and mix well.

Whisk together the shortening, reserved oil and sugar in a bowl. Stir in the garlic, eggs and buttermilk. Add the shortening mixture to the flour mixture and mix well. Pour into a greased 9-inch loaf pan. Bake for 45 to 50 minutes or until a wooden pick inserted in the center comes out clean. Cool in the pan on a wire rack for 5 to 10 minutes. Remove to a wire rack to cool completely.

Roasted Garlic Herb Bread

YIELD: 10 TO 12 SERVINGS

1	cup (2 sticks) unsalted butter
5	garlic cloves, roasted and mashed
1/8	teaspoon red pepper flakes
2	teaspoons kosher salt
1/2	cup finely chopped fresh flat-leaf parsley
1	tablespoon chopped fresh oregano
2	teaspoons chopped fresh dill weed
	Freshly ground black pepper to taste
2	large round loaves crusty bread
3	to 4 tablespoons freshly grated Parmesan cheese

Melt the butter in a saucepan over medium heat. Add the garlic, red pepper and kosher salt and mix well. Remove from the heat and let stand until cool. Stir in the parsley, oregano, dill weed and black pepper to taste.

Cut the loaves of bread into halves horizontally. Brush the cut sides of the bread with half the garlic butter. Let stand for 15 minutes. Grill, cut side down, over hot coals for 2 minutes. Do not leave grill unattended. Turn the bread and brush the cut sides with the remaining garlic butter.

Grill, cut side down, 2 to 3 minutes longer or until golden brown. Cut into wedges, sprinkle with the Parmesan cheese and serve. You may prepare the bread in the oven if preferred. Preheat the oven to 375 degrees. Brush the cut sides of the bread with the garlic butter. Bake, wrapped in foil, for 35 to 40 minutes.

Tropical Oat Bran Muffins

YIELD: 12 LARGE OR 24 SMALL MUFFINS

2	cups flour
3/4	cup whole bran cereal
1/2	cup coconut
2	teaspoons baking powder
1	teaspoon cinnamon
3 1/2	ounces macadamia nuts, coarsely chopped
1/2	cup (1 stick) butter, softened
1	cup sugar
1/4	cup packed brown sugar
3	eggs
3/4	cup mashed ripe bananas (about 2 bananas)
1	(8-ounce) can crushed pineapple, drained
2	teaspoons vanilla extract

Preheat the oven to 350 degrees. Combine the flour, cereal, coconut, baking powder, cinnamon and nuts in a bowl. Cream the butter, sugar and brown sugar in a mixing bowl until light and fluffy. Add the eggs, bananas, pineapple and vanilla and beat until blended. Add to the dry ingredients and mix by hand until blended.

Spoon the batter into 12 large or 24 small greased or paper-lined muffin cups. Bake for 20 to 30 minutes or until a wooden pick inserted in the center comes out clean.

Parmesan Bread Strips

YIELD: 24 BREAD STRIPS

2/3	cup grated Parmesan cheese
1/2	cup finely crushed cornflakes
2	teaspoons minced Italian parsley
1/4	teaspoon garlic salt
	Dash of cayenne pepper
1/2	cup (1 stick) unsalted butter, melted
6	slices sourdough bread

Preheat the oven to 425 degrees. Combine the Parmesan cheese, cornflakes, parsley, garlic salt and cayenne pepper in a shallow dish. Pour the butter into a shallow dish. Trim the crust from the bread and cut each slice into 4 strips. Dip the bread in the butter and roll in the cheese mixture to coat.

Arrange the bread on a foil-lined baking sheet. Bake for 7 minutes or until lightly toasted. Let cool to room temperature. These are best if eaten right away, but they may be stored, tightly wrapped, for up to 2 days.

Cheddar Cheese Popovers

(PICTURED ON PAGE 82)

YIELD: 6 POPOVERS

3	eggs
1 1/4	cups milk
1 1/4	cups sifted flour
1/4	teaspoon salt
3	tablespoons butter, melted
3/4	cup (3 ounces) shredded Cheddar cheese

Preheat the oven to 400 degrees. Beat the eggs in a large mixing bowl until foamy. Add the milk gradually, beating constantly at low speed. Add the flour and salt and beat until smooth. Stir in the butter. Fill 6 generously greased popover cups half full.

Sprinkle evenly with the cheese. Fill with the remaining batter. Bake for 45 to 50 minutes or until brown. Cool in the pan for 1 minute. Remove from the pan and serve hot with softened butter.

Spotlight: Grand Rapids Symphony

Organized all the way back in the 1920s and recognized as one of America's leading regional orchestras, GRS employs almost 100 musicians. Through community outreach, education, and live performance, GRS has touched the hearts and souls of West Michigan. It's the sound of our city.

Blueberry Coffee Cake with Coconut Streusel

(PICTURED ON PAGE 82)

YIELD: 12 SERVINGS

(PICTURED ON PAGE 82)

Feeling blue?

Michigan produces

more blueberries

than any other state.

So Michigan cooks

know how to prevent

batter from turning

blue: just coat the

berries with flour

before adding them

to the mix!

Coconut Streusel

1	cup sweetened flaked coconut
1/2	cup packed brown sugar
1/3	cup flour
1	teaspoon cinnamon
1/4	cup (1/2 stick) unsalted butter, softened

Coffee Cake

2	cups flour
2 1/2	teaspoons baking powder
1/2	teaspoon salt
1/2	cup (1 stick) butter, softened
1	cup sugar
2	eggs
1	cup milk
2 1/2	cups fresh blueberries, or 12 ounces frozen blueberries, thawed

For the streusel, combine the coconut, brown sugar, flour and cinnamon in a bowl. Cut in the butter until crumbly.

For the coffee cake, preheat the oven to 375 degrees. Sift the flour, baking powder and salt together into a small bowl. Cream the butter in a mixing bowl until light and fluffy. Add the sugar gradually, beating until blended. Add the eggs, 1 at a time, beating well after each addition. Add the dry ingredients alternately with the milk, mixing well after each addition. Fold in the blueberries.

Spoon the batter into a greased and floured 9×13-inch baking pan. Sprinkle the streusel evenly over the batter. Bake for 35 minutes or until a wooden pick inserted in the center comes out clean and the topping is golden brown. Cool slightly on a wire rack. Serve warm.

Cinnamon Cream Cheese Coffee Cake

This coffee cake freezes well after baked; warm slightly prior to serving.

YIELD: 8 SERVINGS

Topping

1	cup flour
1	cup sugar
2	teaspoons cinnamon
½	cup (1 stick) cold butter

Coffee Cake

2	cups sifted flour
2	teaspoons baking powder
½	teaspoon baking soda
½	teaspoon salt
½	cup (1 stick) butter, softened
8	ounces cream cheese, softened
1¼	cups sugar
2	eggs
1	teaspoon vanilla extract
½	cup milk

For the topping, combine the flour, sugar and cinnamon in a bowl. Cut in the butter using a pastry blender until crumbly.

For the coffee cake, preheat the oven to 350 degrees. Combine the flour, baking powder, baking soda and salt in a small bowl. Cream the butter, cream cheese, sugar, eggs and vanilla in a mixing bowl until light and fluffy.

Add the flour mixture alternately with the milk, mixing well after each addition. Pour the batter into a greased 9×13-inch baking pan. Sprinkle with the topping. Bake for 35 to 40 minutes or until golden brown on top. Serve warm.

King's Pancakes with Fresh Peach Sauce

King's Pancakes were adapted by Josef Huber, C.M.C., Executive Chef, Amway Grand Plaza. Fit for serving to royalty or to the family, these pancakes like to mix it up a little!

YIELD: 4 SERVINGS

Some like 'em scrambled.

Americans like their pancakes light and fluffy. The French prepare them paper-thin. Belgians prefer a hearty waffle. And Germans? They're fond of the scramble. Yes, scrambled pancakes. Hey, don't knock 'em 'til you try 'em!

Fresh Peach Sauce

2	large ripe peaches, peeled and sliced
1	teaspoon grated orange zest
	Juice of 1/2 orange
2	tablespoons dry white wine
2	teaspoons fresh lemon juice
1/4	cup sugar
1/2	teaspoon cinnamon

Pancakes

6	egg yolks
1 1/3	cups flour
1	cup milk
1/2	teaspoon salt
6	egg whites
1/4	cup sugar
1/4	cup (1/2 stick) butter
1/2	cup raisins
	Sliced peaches
	Confectioners' sugar

For the sauce, bring the peaches, orange zest, orange juice, wine, lemon juice, sugar and cinnamon to a boil in a medium saucepan. Cook for 5 minutes, stirring frequently. Remove from the heat and let sit, covered with foil, for 10 minutes. Pour the mixture into a blender and process until blended.

For the pancakes, combine the egg yolks, flour, milk and salt in a bowl and mix well. Beat the egg whites in a mixing bowl until soft peaks form. Add the sugar and beat until stiff peaks form. Fold the egg white mixture into the egg yolk mixture.

Melt the butter in a large nonstick pan over medium heat. Pour the batter into the pan and sprinkle with the raisins. Cook until the pancake begins to set. Stir the batter using 2 forks. Cook until set, stirring frequently. Divide evenly among 4 plates. Top with the peach sauce and peach slices. Sprinkle with confectioners' sugar.

Oven Puff Pancake with Cinnamon Rhubarb Compote

YIELD: 4 TO 6 SERVINGS

Cinnamon Rhubarb Compote

¼	cup sugar
1	cinnamon stick
1	tablespoon minced fresh gingerroot
½	cup orange juice
3	to 4 cups coarsely chopped rhubarb

Pancake

3	eggs, slightly beaten
¾	cup milk
¾	cup flour
1	tablespoon sugar
¼	cup (½ stick) butter
	Confectioners' sugar

For the compote, bring the sugar, cinnamon stick, gingerroot and orange juice to a boil in a large heavy saucepan over medium heat, stirring constantly until the sugar dissolves. Add the rhubarb and return to a boil. Reduce the heat and simmer for 4 minutes or until the fruit is tender but not falling apart, stirring occasionally. Remove from the heat. Let cool to room temperature and remove the cinnamon stick. Warm the compote before serving.

For the pancake, preheat the oven to 425 degrees. Whisk together the eggs, milk, flour and sugar in a medium bowl. The batter will have small lumps. Melt the butter in a 10-inch ovenproof skillet in the oven. Pour the batter into the prepared skillet. Bake for 18 to 20 minutes or until the edges are puffy and golden brown. Sprinkle lightly with confectioners' sugar. Cut into wedges and serve with the warm compote.

Baked French Toast with Berries

(PICTURED ON PAGE 83)

YIELD: 8 SERVINGS

3	eggs
1	tablespoon sugar
1	teaspoon vanilla extract
1½	cups milk
10	slices English muffin bread
½	cup flour
2	tablespoons packed brown sugar
½	teaspoon cinnamon
¼	cup (½ stick) butter
1	cup fresh or thawed frozen blueberries
1	cup sliced strawberries
	Confectioners' sugar

Combine the eggs, sugar and vanilla in a mixing bowl and beat until blended. Stir in the milk. Arrange 5 slices of bread in a 9×13-inch glass baking dish sprayed with nonstick cooking spray. Pour half the egg mixture over the bread slices, turning to coat. Arrange the remaining bread slices over the prepared layer. Pour the remaining egg mixture over the top. Chill, covered with plastic wrap, for 8 hours. Let stand at room temperature for 30 minutes before baking.

Preheat the oven to 375 degrees. Combine the flour, brown sugar and cinnamon in a bowl. Cut in the butter until crumbly. Lift the top bread layer with a spatula and sprinkle the blueberries over the bottom layer. Replace the top layer and sprinkle with the cinnamon mixture. Bake for 35 minutes or until puffy and golden brown. Sprinkle with the strawberries and confectioners' sugar. Serve warm.

Festive Brunch Fruit Salad

YIELD: 10 TO 12 SERVINGS

1	cup green grapes
1	cup raspberries
1	cup cantaloupe balls
2	cups sliced strawberries
2	peaches, sliced
2	plums, sliced
2	kiwifruit, sliced
1	orange, separated into segments
½	cup orange juice
½	cup orange liqueur such as Grand Marnier
	Sugar to taste (optional)

Combine the grapes, raspberries, cantaloupe, strawberries, peaches, plums, kiwifruit, orange, orange juice and orange liqueur in a large bowl and toss gently. Sprinkle with sugar. Chill, covered, for 2 to 8 hours.

Winter Morning Fruit Salad

YIELD: 12 TO 14 SERVINGS

2	tablespoons butter
4	cups thinly sliced peeled peaches
⅔	cup sugar
3	tablespoons cornstarch
1	teaspoon cinnamon
1¼	cups water
1	tablespoon fresh lemon juice
2	(11-ounce) cans mandarin oranges, drained
3	cups cubed fresh pineapple
4	cups fresh or thawed frozen strawberry halves
4	bananas, thinly sliced
1	large crisp apple, peeled and thinly sliced

Melt the butter in a large heavy skillet over medium-high heat. Add the peaches and sauté for 4 minutes, stirring gently. Combine the sugar, cornstarch and cinnamon in a large saucepan. Add the water and mix well. Stir in the peaches. Cook over medium heat for 8 to 10 minutes or until the liquid thickens and is clear. Remove from the heat and stir in the lemon juice. Let stand until cool.

Combine the mandarin oranges, pineapple and strawberries in a large bowl. Pour the peach mixture over the fruit and stir gently to combine. Chill, covered, for 8 hours. Add the bananas and apple and toss gently to combine just before serving.

Cheese and Sausage Strudel

This recipe is good for a large group as it multiplies well. Can be made a day in advance and baked just before serving.

YIELD: 6 STRUDEL

A Grand Haven, indeed.

Michigan's inland lakes and rivers eventually meet the Great Lakes, forming beautiful channels and harbors. Enter Grand Haven, a year-round tourist mecca. Punctuated by a mile-long waterfront walkway and a pier housing a pair of 1900s-era lighthouses, the city also features a charming downtown, the "world's largest musical fountain," an annual Coast Guard Festival, a January Winterfest, and a beautiful sandy beach.

Cheese Sauce

2	tablespoons butter
2½	tablespoons flour
1¼	cups milk
½	cup (2 ounces) shredded Swiss or Gruyère cheese
3	tablespoons grated Parmesan cheese
½	teaspoon salt
⅛	to ¼ teaspoon cayenne pepper, or to taste

Sausage and Egg Filling

⅓	pound bulk pork sausage
6	eggs, slightly beaten
½	teaspoon thyme
1	tablespoon parsley

Assembly

6	sheets frozen phyllo dough, thawed
½	cup (1 stick) butter, melted

For the sauce, melt the butter in a small saucepan. Whisk in the flour. Cook over medium heat until bubbly, whisking constantly. Add the milk gradually, stirring constantly. Bring to a boil and boil for 1 minute, stirring constantly. Add the cheeses and stir until blended. Add the salt and cayenne pepper and mix well. Remove from the heat.

For the filling, brown the sausage in a skillet, stirring until crumbly; drain. Add the eggs and thyme and mix well. Cook over medium heat until the eggs are set, stirring frequently. Stir in the parsley and cheese sauce. Remove from the heat and let stand until cool.

To assemble, preheat the oven to 375 degrees. Unfold the phyllo dough. Cover with a paper towel topped with a clean damp kitchen towel. Lay 1 phyllo sheet on a work surface and brush with some of the melted butter. Fold in half lengthwise and brush with melted butter. Spoon ⅙ of the filling along 1 short edge of the phyllo, leaving a border. Fold the border over the filling. Fold in the long edges of the phyllo and roll from the short edge to enclose the filling. Place seam side down on an ungreased baking sheet. Brush the top with melted butter. Repeat the procedure with the remaining phyllo sheets, butter and filling. Bake for 15 minutes or until crisp and light brown. Serve hot. Uncooked strudel may be stored, covered, in the refrigerator overnight. Bring to room temperature before baking.

Frittata with Tomatoes and Basil

YIELD: 4 TO 6 SERVINGS

6	eggs
6	egg whites
¼	cup heavy cream
1½	cups (6 ounces) crumbled feta cheese
10	oil-pack sun-dried tomatoes, finely chopped
1	small shallot, minced
⅓	cup fresh basil leaves, finely chopped
2	to 3 drops hot pepper sauce
½	to 1 teaspoon salt
¼	teaspoon freshly ground pepper
3	tablespoons butter
¼	cup (1 ounce) freshly grated asiago cheese

Preheat the broiler. Whisk the eggs, egg whites and heavy cream in a large bowl until blended. Stir in the feta cheese, tomatoes, shallot, basil, hot pepper sauce, salt and pepper. Melt the butter in a cast-iron skillet over medium-high heat. Pour in the egg mixture. Do not stir.

Cook for 5 minutes or until the side and bottom begin to brown, lifting the edges to let uncooked portions come into contact with the skillet. Sprinkle with the asiago cheese. Broil for 2 minutes or until the eggs begin to puff and the cheese is brown. Remove from the skillet, cut into wedges and serve warm or at room temperature.

Venetian Quiche

(PICTURED ON PAGE 84)

YIELD: 6 SERVINGS

2	tablespoons butter
1	garlic clove, minced
1½	cups sliced fresh button mushrooms
1	baked (9-inch) pie shell
8	ounces (2 cups) shredded Italian cheese blend
4	eggs
1½	cups half-and-half
1	tablespoon chopped fresh parsley
1	tablespoon chopped fresh basil
½	teaspoon salt
½	teaspoon freshly ground pepper

Preheat the oven to 425 degrees. Melt the butter in a large skillet over medium heat. Add the garlic and mushrooms and sauté for 7 to 10 minutes or until the mushrooms are soft. Arrange the mixture over the bottom of the pie shell. Sprinkle with the cheese.

Combine the eggs, half-and-half, parsley, basil, salt and pepper in a bowl and whisk until blended. Pour over the cheese layer. Bake for 40 to 50 minutes or until the crust is golden brown and the eggs are set in the center. Let cool slightly.

Spinach and Cheese Strata with Sourdough

(PICTURED ON PAGE 82)

YIELD: 10 SERVINGS

1	tablespoon olive oil
1	pound fresh spinach, trimmed and coarsely chopped
6	tablespoons butter
2	large onions, finely chopped
1	teaspoon kosher salt
1/2	teaspoon freshly ground pepper
1/4	teaspoon freshly grated nutmeg
1	pound bulk pork sausage, cooked and drained (optional)
8	cups cubed sourdough bread with crusts removed
2	cups (about 6 ounces) shredded Gruyère cheese
1	cup (about 2 ounces) finely grated Parmigiano-Reggiano cheese
2 3/4	cups milk
9	eggs
2	tablespoons Dijon mustard
1/2	teaspoon salt
1/2	teaspoon freshly ground pepper

Heat the olive oil in a large sauté pan over medium-high heat. Add the spinach and cook until wilted, stirring occasionally. Melt the butter in a large heavy skillet over medium heat. Add the onions and cook for 5 minutes or until soft, stirring frequently. Add 1 teaspoon salt, 1/2 teaspoon pepper and the nutmeg. Cook for 1 minute, stirring constantly. Add the spinach and sausage and mix well. Remove from the heat.

Arrange 1/3 of the bread cubes in a buttered shallow non-metal 4-quart baking dish. Spread 1/3 of the spinach mixture evenly over the bread. Sprinkle with 1/3 of the Gruyère cheese and 1/3 of the Parmigiano-Reggiano cheese.

Repeat the layers 2 more times, ending with the cheese layers. Combine the milk, eggs, mustard, 1/2 teaspoon salt and 1/2 teaspoon pepper in a large bowl and whisk until blended. Pour over the prepared layers. Chill, covered in plastic wrap, for 8 hours or longer.

Preheat the oven to 350 degrees. Let the dish stand at room temperature for 30 minutes before baking. Bake for 50 to 55 minutes or until puffed, golden brown and cooked through. Remove from the oven and let stand for 5 minutes before serving.

Spotlight: Sleeping Bear Dunes

This 35-mile stretch of towering sands overlooks North and South Manitou Islands. Legend has it the area was created when a mother bear and her cubs swam across Lake Michigan to escape a forest fire. The cubs didn't make it and were transformed into the Islands. Their mother still waits for them on shore. The Great Spirit has covered her with sand to warm and comfort her.

Cheese-Filled Crepes with Spiced Rum Sauce

YIELD: 8 CREPES

Crepes

2	eggs
1/2	teaspoon salt
1	cup flour, sifted
1	cup milk
	Butter

Filling

8	ounces cream cheese, softened
16	ounces ricotta cheese, at room temperature
1	egg, slightly beaten
1	tablespoon sugar
1/4	teaspoon salt

Spiced Rum Sauce

1	cup sour cream
2	tablespoons brown sugar
1	tablespoon spiced rum
1/2	teaspoon vanilla extract
1/2	teaspoon cinnamon

For the crepes, combine the eggs and salt in a bowl and whisk well. Add the flour alternately with the milk, whisking until smooth. Melt butter to coat the bottom of a large skillet over medium heat. Pour 2 to 3 tablespoons of the batter into the skillet. Tilt the skillet immediately to let the batter spread over the bottom of the skillet. Cook for 30 seconds. Remove the crepe from the skillet and place on a paper towel, cooked side up. Repeat the process with the remaining batter, adding additional butter as needed. Stack the crepes alternately with paper towels.

For the filling, combine the cream cheese and ricotta cheese in a bowl and beat until blended. Add the egg and mix until smooth. Add the sugar and salt and mix well. Place a rounded tablespoon of filling on the cooked side of each crepe. Fold the sides over to enclose the filling. Arrange the filled crepes, seam side down, on a plastic wrap-lined platter. Chill, covered, until ready to serve.

For the sauce, combine the sour cream, brown sugar, rum, vanilla and cinnamon in a microwave-safe bowl and mix well. Microwave for 60 seconds or until the brown sugar is dissolved and the sauce is warm.

To serve, melt 2 to 3 tablespoons butter in a skillet over medium heat. Cook the crepes in the butter until the filling is warm and the crepes are golden brown on all sides, turning once. Serve warm with the Spiced Rum Sauce.

Side Dishes

Above: Green Beans with Caramelized Onions (page 111). Opposite page from top to bottom: Glazed Corn on the Cob (page 108), Ginger Fried Rice (page 121), Northwoods Wild Rice (page 118), Barbecued Baked Beans (page 106), Tomato Dijon Tart (page 116), Spinach Parmesan Tomatoes (page 116).

Beijing Asparagus

YIELD: 6 TO 8 SERVINGS

2	tablespoons soy sauce
1	tablespoon sesame oil
1	tablespoon sliced gingerroot
2	bunches asparagus, trimmed
1	tablespoon sesame seeds

Whisk together the soy sauce, sesame oil and gingerroot in a wide shallow dish. Let stand for 15 minutes. Combine the asparagus with 1/2 cup water in a microwave-safe dish and cover with a paper towel. Microwave on High for 6 minutes. Rotate the dish 1/4 turn and microwave on High for 4 minutes. Plunge the asparagus in cold water to stop the cooking process; drain.

Add the asparagus to the soy sauce mixture and turn several times to coat well. Remove the asparagus to a plate and chill, covered with plastic wrap, for 4 hours or longer. Sprinkle with the sesame seeds before serving.

Roasted Asparagus

YIELD: 6 SERVINGS

2	pounds asparagus, trimmed
	Salt and freshly ground pepper to taste
2	tablespoons butter
2	teaspoons soy sauce
1 1/2	teaspoons balsamic vinegar

Preheat the oven to 400 degrees. Place the asparagus in a single layer on a baking sheet lined with foil. Spray the asparagus generously with cooking spray. Season with salt and pepper. Bake for 11 to 13 minutes or until tender. Remove the asparagus to a serving dish.

Melt the butter in a small saucepan over medium heat. Cook the butter until light brown, stirring constantly. Be careful not to burn the butter. Remove from the heat and stir in the soy sauce and vinegar. Drizzle over the asparagus.

Look who's stalking. One of the first signs of spring is the appearance of fresh asparagus in the markets. These long, green stalks—low in calories, high in nutrients—are one of nature's most perfect foods. When buying, look for firm spears with closed, compact tips.

Barbecued Baked Beans

(PICTURED ON PAGE 102)

YIELD: 12 TO 14 SERVINGS

1	(48-ounce) jar Great Northern beans
1½	pounds pork loin, cubed
¼	large sweet onion, chopped
½	to 1 teaspoon salt
	Freshly ground pepper to taste
1	(14-ounce) bottle ketchup
3	tablespoons mustard
1½	cups packed brown sugar

Preheat the oven to 300 degrees. Combine the beans, pork, onion, salt, pepper, ketchup, mustard and brown sugar in a large bowl and mix well. Spoon into a non-reactive 3-quart baking dish sprayed with cooking spray.

Bake for 5 to 6 hours, stirring every 30 minutes. You may bake at 325 degrees for 4 hours if preferred.

Mexican Beans with Cilantro

YIELD: 6 TO 8 SERVINGS

1	tablespoon vegetable oil
1	small onion, chopped
1	garlic clove, minced
2	(15-ounce) cans black beans, drained and rinsed
1	(15-ounce) can corn, drained
1	(16-ounce) jar salsa
¼	to ½ cup chopped fresh cilantro
1	small jalapeño chile, seeded and minced

Heat the oil in a large skillet over medium heat. Add the onion and garlic and sauté for 5 to 7 minutes or until tender.

Add the beans, corn, salsa, cilantro and chile and mix well. Cook for 5 minutes or until heated through. Serve immediately.

Broccoli with Goat Cheese Sauce

This Indian-inspired dish benefits from toasted spices and offers a light, but sophisticated, alternative to traditional cheese sauce.

YIELD: 4 TO 6 SERVINGS

1	teaspoon cumin
½	teaspoon cayenne pepper
½	teaspoon kosher salt
¼	teaspoon turmeric
3	hard-cooked egg yolks
8	ounces goat cheese, softened
⅓	cup olive oil
¼	cup water
1	tablespoon fresh lemon juice
1½	to 2 pounds broccoli spears

Combine the cumin, cayenne pepper, kosher salt and turmeric in a heavy skillet over medium heat. Cook for 2 to 3 minutes or until the spices begin to darken, stirring frequently. Remove from the heat and let stand until cool. Process the egg yolks, goat cheese, olive oil, water, lemon juice and spice blend in a blender until smooth. Adjust the salt to taste.

Steam the broccoli over boiling water for 5 minutes or until tender-crisp. Remove to a serving platter. Drizzle lightly with the cheese sauce. Serve immediately.

Brussels Sprouts with Bacon and Garlic

YIELD: 6 SERVINGS

3	slices bacon, cut into ½-inch pieces
3	garlic cloves, thinly sliced
1	tablespoon unsalted butter
1	pound Brussels sprouts, trimmed and halved lengthwise
	Kosher salt to taste
1	tablespoon unsalted butter
¼	cup pine nuts
	Freshly ground pepper to taste

Cook the bacon in a heavy 10-inch skillet until nearly crisp. Add the garlic and cook until the garlic is light golden brown and the bacon is crisp, stirring frequently. Remove with a slotted spoon to a small bowl. Drain all but 2 tablespoons of the drippings. Add 1 tablespoon butter to the reserved drippings and melt the butter over low heat, stirring frequently. Arrange the Brussels sprouts, cut side down, in a single layer in the skillet. Season with kosher salt.

Cook for 12 to 15 minutes or until the cut sides are golden brown. Do not turn. Remove the Brussels sprouts to a serving bowl. Melt 1 tablespoon butter in the skillet over medium heat, stirring constantly. Add the pine nuts and cook for 3 to 4 minutes or until golden, stirring constantly. Add the bacon and garlic and cook until heated through. Spoon over the Brussels sprouts. Season with pepper.

Carrot Soufflé

YIELD: 6 SERVINGS

2½	cups coarsely chopped carrots
2/3	cup sugar
3	eggs
1	tablespoon flour
1	teaspoon baking powder
1	teaspoon salt
¼	teaspoon cinnamon
1	cup milk
½	cup (1 stick) butter

Preheat the oven to 375 degrees. Combine the carrots with enough water to cover in a heavy 2-quart saucepan. Simmer, covered, for 10 to 12 minutes or until tender; drain.

Process the carrots, sugar, eggs, flour, baking powder, salt, cinnamon, milk and butter in a blender or food processor until smooth. Pour into a greased 2-quart soufflé dish. Bake for 45 minutes or until set in the center.

Glazed Corn on the Cob

(PICTURED ON PAGE 102)

Grilling the corn provides a wonderful caramelization of the maple chipotle glaze.

YIELD: 6 SERVINGS

½	cup pure maple syrup
¼	cup (½ stick) butter
2	to 3 garlic cloves, minced
4	teaspoons minced chipotle chiles in adobo sauce
¼	teaspoon kosher salt
6	ears fresh sweet corn

Combine the maple syrup, butter, garlic, chiles and kosher salt in a small heavy saucepan. Simmer for 10 to 12 minutes, stirring occasionally. You may prepare the glaze to this point and chill, covered, for 1 day. Reheat before using.

Brush the corn generously with the glaze. Grill over medium-hot coals for 8 minutes or until the corn begins to turn brown, turning frequently. Remove to a serving platter and serve with the remaining glaze on the side.

Southwest Cheddar-Jack Corn Pudding

YIELD: 12 SERVINGS

Corn Bread

1	cup yellow cornmeal
1	cup flour
1/4	cup sugar
4	teaspoons baking powder
1	teaspoon salt
1/4	cup (1/2 stick) unsalted butter, melted and cooled
1	cup milk
4	ounces (1 cup) shredded sharp Cheddar cheese
1	(4-ounce) can chopped green chiles
2	eggs

Pudding

2	cups fresh or frozen thawed corn
8	ounces (2 cups) shredded Pepper Jack cheese
1	red bell pepper, chopped
1/2	cup chopped green onions
1	tablespoon chopped fresh cilantro
2	cups buttermilk
1	cup enchilada sauce
6	eggs
1/2	teaspoon salt
1/2	cup (2 ounces) shredded sharp Cheddar cheese

For the corn bread, preheat the oven to 425 degrees. Sift the cornmeal, flour, sugar, baking powder and salt into a large bowl. Whisk together the butter, milk, cheese, chiles and eggs in a small bowl. Add to the cornmeal mixture and stir just until combined. Pour the batter into a greased 8-inch square baking pan. Bake for 20 minutes or until light golden brown. Let cool on a wire rack for 5 minutes. Invert the corn bread onto the wire rack and cool completely.

For the pudding, allow the corn to drain in a strainer for 10 minutes. Press the corn gently with paper towels to remove any excess moisture. Crumble the cornbread into a large bowl. Add the corn, Pepper Jack cheese, bell pepper, green onions and cilantro and mix well.

Whisk the buttermilk, enchilada sauce, eggs and salt in a bowl until blended. Pour over the corn mixture and toss gently to combine. Spoon the mixture into a buttered non-reactive 9×13-inch baking dish. Chill, covered, for 1 to 24 hours.

Preheat the oven to 350 degrees. Bake the corn pudding for 30 minutes. Sprinkle with the Cheddar cheese. Bake for an additional 30 minutes or until golden brown. Remove from the oven and let stand for 10 minutes. Serve warm.

Caponata Siciliano

YIELD: 8 TO 10 SERVINGS

1	(1¼- to 1½-pound) eggplant
1	teaspoon salt
½	cup olive oil
1½	cups coarsely chopped onions
1	cup chopped celery
1	cup chopped tomatoes
1	teaspoon freshly ground black pepper
½	teaspoon salt
2	tablespoons tomato paste
24	small pitted black olives
½	cup capers
½	teaspoon red pepper flakes
2	tablespoons chopped fresh basil

Cut the eggplant into 1-inch pieces. Sprinkle with 1 teaspoon salt. Heat the olive oil in a large skillet over medium heat. Add the eggplant and cook for 8 to 10 minutes or until brown, turning gently. Remove with a slotted spoon to a bowl and let stand until cool. Cook the onions and celery in the skillet for 5 to 7 minutes or until the onion is softened, stirring frequently.

Reduce the heat to low and add the eggplant, tomatoes, black pepper and ½ teaspoon salt and mix well. Cook, covered, for 5 minutes. Stir in the tomato paste, black olives, capers, red pepper and basil. Cook, covered, for 5 minutes. Remove from the heat and let cool. Adjust the seasonings to taste. Chill, covered, for 1 to 2 days. Bring to room temperature before serving. Garnish with lemon slices.

Green Beans with Caramelized Onions

(PICTURED ON PAGE 103)

YIELD: 4 SERVINGS

1	pound green beans, trimmed
2	sweet onions
2	tablespoons butter
2	tablespoons packed brown sugar
1	to 2 teaspoons balsamic vinegar

Bring enough salted water to cover the green beans to a boil in a saucepan. Add the green beans and cook for 10 minutes; drain. Chill, covered, in the refrigerator up to 1 day.

Cut the onions into thin slices and cut each slice in half. Cook the onions over medium-high heat in a large nonstick skillet for 8 to 10 minutes or until softened. Do not stir. Cook for 5 to 10 minutes or until golden brown, stirring frequently. Reduce the heat to medium and stir in the butter and brown sugar. Add the vinegar and mix well. Add the green beans and cook for 5 minutes or until heated through.

Spicy Green Beans

YIELD: 6 SERVINGS

1	pound green beans, trimmed
3/4	teaspoon cornstarch
1 1/2	teaspoons water
2	tablespoons soy sauce
2	tablespoons rice vinegar
2	tablespoons sesame oil
1	tablespoon vegetable oil
1/2	teaspoon chili oil
2	teaspoons minced garlic
1	teaspoon sugar
1/2	teaspoon red pepper flakes

Bring 4 cups salted water to a boil in a medium saucepan. Add the green beans. Cook for 6 to 8 minutes or until tender-crisp; drain. Remove the green beans to a bowl.

Combine the cornstarch and 1 1/2 teaspoons water in a small bowl and mix well. Combine with the soy sauce, vinegar, sesame oil, vegetable oil, chili oil, garlic, sugar and red pepper in a small saucepan.

Bring to a boil over medium-high heat. Cook for 2 to 3 minutes or until slightly thickened, stirring constantly. Pour the sauce over the green beans and toss to coat. Serve warm or at room temperature.

Greek Potatoes

(PICTURED ON PAGE 104)

YIELD: 6 SERVINGS

2	tablespoons butter
2	tablespoons olive oil
8	small new red potatoes, halved
1	tablespoon fresh lemon juice
2	to 3 teaspoons chopped fresh oregano
1	tablespoon chopped fresh parsley
1	teaspoon salt
¼	teaspoon freshly ground pepper

Heat the butter and olive oil in a large skillet over medium-high heat. Add the potatoes and sprinkle with the lemon juice. Cook the potatoes for 5 to 7 minutes or until brown, turning occasionally.

Reduce the heat to low and cook, covered, for 15 to 20 minutes or until the potatoes are tender. Sprinkle with the oregano, parsley, salt and pepper and serve.

Trio of Roasted Potatoes

This dish is best when made as an accompaniment to turkey or other roasted meats.

YIELD: 6 TO 8 SERVINGS

1	tablespoon olive oil
1½	pounds (about 3 cups) russet potatoes, peeled and cut into 1-inch pieces
1	pound (about 2 cups) Yukon gold potatoes, peeled and cut into 1-inch pieces
1	pound (about 2 cups) red potatoes, cut into 1-inch pieces
¼	cup olive oil
3	tablespoons finely chopped fresh herbs, such as basil, marjoram, sage and thyme
2	tablespoons chopped garlic
	Kosher salt and freshly ground pepper to taste

Preheat the oven to 400 degrees. Line a rimmed baking sheet with foil and coat with 1 tablespoon olive oil. Combine the potatoes, ¼ cup olive oil, herbs and garlic in a bowl and toss to coat. Season with kosher salt and pepper. Spoon the potatoes onto the prepared baking sheet.

Roast the potatoes for 75 minutes or until golden brown and tender, stirring occasionally. Remove the potatoes to a bowl and serve immediately. You may use ¼ cup of pan drippings from roasted meat such as chicken, turkey or roast beef in place of the ¼ cup olive oil if desired.

Smashed Potatoes with Bacon and Cheese

YIELD: 6 TO 8 SERVINGS

3	pounds red potatoes
1	teaspoon kosher salt
1	cup half-and-half
½	cup (1 stick) unsalted butter
½	cup sour cream
¾	cup (3 ounces) shredded white Cheddar cheese
3	slices bacon, crisp-cooked and crumbled
2	teaspoons kosher salt
1	teaspoon freshly ground pepper

Combine the potatoes and 1 teaspoon kosher salt with enough cold water to cover in a 4-quart saucepan. Bring to a boil. Reduce the heat and simmer, covered, for 25 to 35 minutes or until the potatoes are tender; drain. Place the potatoes in a large mixing bowl. Combine the half-and-half and butter in a small saucepan over medium heat. Cook until the butter is melted, stirring frequently. Remove from the heat.

Beat the potatoes on low using an electric mixer fitted with a paddle attachment. Add the half-and-half mixture gradually, beating on low constantly. Fold in the sour cream, cheese, bacon, 2 teaspoons kosher salt and pepper with a wooden spoon. Serve immediately or keep warm in a 200-degree oven.

Great water.
Michigan has more miles of freshwater shoreline than any other state in the nation. In fact, the state's name comes from the Indian phrase "michi gami"— meaning "the great water."

Stuffed Baked Potatoes with Rosemary

YIELD: 6 SERVINGS

6	large baking potatoes
1/3	cup sour cream
1/4	cup (1 ounce) crumbled Stilton cheese or Gorgonzola cheese
6	tablespoons butter, softened
2	large garlic cloves, minced
1 1/2	teaspoons chopped fresh rosemary
	Kosher salt and freshly ground pepper to taste
1/3	cup sour cream
1/4	cup (1 ounce) crumbled Stilton cheese or Gorgonzola cheese

Preheat the oven to 400 degrees. Pierce the potatoes several times with a fork and wrap in foil. Bake for 45 minutes. Remove the foil and bake for 30 minutes or until cooked through. Remove from the oven and let cool slightly. Slice off the top third of each potato. Scoop the pulp from the bottom 2/3 of the potatoes into a medium bowl, leaving a 1/4-inch shell. Arrange the potato shells on a baking sheet. Scoop the pulp from the top 1/3 of the potatoes into the bowl and discard the peels.

Combine 1/3 cup sour cream, 1/4 cup cheese, the butter, garlic and rosemary with the pulp and beat until blended. Season with kosher salt and pepper. Spoon the potato mixture into the shells. You may prepare to this point 1 day in advance. Store, covered, in the refrigerator. Let stand at room temperature for 30 minutes before baking.

Preheat the oven to 400 degrees. Bake the potatoes for 25 to 30 minutes or until light brown and heated through. Combine 1/3 cup sour cream and 1/4 cup cheese in a small bowl and mix well. Place a dollop of the sour cream mixture on each potato and serve immediately.

Spinach with Three Cheeses

YIELD: 6 SERVINGS

½	cup toasted bread crumbs
3	tablespoons butter
1	onion, chopped
2	garlic cloves, chopped
1	(10-ounce) package frozen chopped spinach, thawed and squeezed dry
½	teaspoon salt
½	teaspoon freshly ground pepper
¼	teaspoon freshly ground nutmeg
15	ounces ricotta cheese
8	ounces (2 cups) shredded mozzarella cheese
⅔	cup freshly grated Parmesan cheese
3	eggs, beaten
2	tablespoons toasted pine nuts

Preheat the oven to 350 degrees. Sprinkle the bread crumbs over the bottom of an 8x8-inch non-reactive baking dish sprayed generously with cooking spray. Melt the butter in a large heavy skillet over medium heat. Add the onion and sauté for 5 minutes. Add the garlic and sauté for 3 minutes or until the onion is tender. Add the spinach, salt, pepper and nutmeg and sauté for 3 minutes or until the liquid from the spinach evaporates.

Combine the ricotta cheese, mozzarella cheese and Parmesan cheese in a large bowl. Add the eggs and mix well. Add the spinach mixture and stir until blended. Pour into the prepared baking dish. Sprinkle with the pine nuts. Bake for 40 to 50 minutes or until the filling is set in the center and the top is brown. Let stand for 10 minutes before serving.

Spinach Parmesan Tomatoes

(PICTURED ON PAGE 102)

YIELD: 12 SERVINGS

2	(10-ounce) packages frozen chopped spinach
1	cup soft bread crumbs
1	cup seasoned bread crumbs
1	small garlic clove, minced
1	cup chopped green onions
6	eggs, slightly beaten
3/4	cup (1 1/2 sticks) butter, melted
1/2	cup (2 ounces) freshly grated Parmesan cheese
1	teaspoon thyme
3/4	teaspoon salt
12	thick tomato slices

Cook the spinach using the package directions; drain and squeeze out the excess liquid. Combine with the bread crumbs, garlic, green onions, eggs, butter, Parmesan cheese, thyme and salt in a bowl and mix well. Preheat the oven to 350 degrees. Arrange the tomatoes in a single layer on a greased baking sheet. Mound an equal amount of the spinach mixture on each tomato slice.

You may prepare to this point and chill, covered, in the refrigerator. Let stand for 30 minutes before baking. Bake for 15 minutes or until the spinach is set and beginning to brown. Arrange on a serving platter and serve immediately.

Tomato Dijon Tart

(PICTURED ON PAGE 102)

YIELD: 6 SERVINGS

6	large Roma tomatoes
3	tablespoons honey Dijon mustard
1/2	cup chopped fresh basil
1	unbaked (9-inch) pie shell
8	ounces (2 cups) shredded mozzarella cheese
2	tablespoons packed brown sugar
	Salt and freshly ground pepper to taste

Preheat the oven to 425 degrees. Cut the tomatoes into 1/4-inch-thick slices. Place on paper towels to drain. Combine the mustard and basil in a small bowl and mix well. Spread over the bottom of the pie shell. Layer with half the cheese, the tomatoes and remaining cheese.

Sprinkle with the brown sugar, salt and pepper. Bake for 15 to 20 minutes or until the crust is golden brown, the cheese is melted and the tomatoes are tender. Garnish with basil leaves. Cut into wedges and serve warm.

Roasted Butternut Squash with Cinnamon Glazed Onions

YIELD: 4 SERVINGS

2	pounds winter squash, cut into 2-inch pieces
1/3	cup raisins
3	tablespoons vegetable oil
1/4	cup sliced almonds
2	extra large sweet onions, thinly sliced
1/4	cup sugar
1 1/2	teaspoons cinnamon
1/4	cup (1 ounce) freshly grated Parmesan cheese
2	teaspoons minced fresh herbs, such as rosemary, thyme and marjoram
	Kosher salt and freshly ground pepper to taste

Preheat the oven to 375 degrees. Place the squash in a baking dish. Bake for 50 to 60 minutes or until tender. Combine the raisins with water to cover in a small bowl. Let stand until the raisins are plump; drain. Heat the oil in a skillet over medium-high heat. Add the almonds and sauté for 3 to 4 minutes or until golden. Remove with a slotted spoon to paper towels to drain. Cook the onions in the skillet over medium-high heat for 8 to 10 minutes or until soft, stirring occasionally.

Reduce the heat to medium and add the sugar and cinnamon. Cook for 20 to 25 minutes or until the onions are brown, stirring occasionally. Add the raisins, Parmesan cheese, herbs, kosher salt and pepper and mix well. Cook until heated through, stirring frequently. Add the squash and stir gently. Spoon into a serving dish. Sprinkle with the almonds.

Northwoods Wild Rice

(PICTURED ON PAGE 102)

Pamper yourself with the nutty flavor of pure wild rice, available from supermarkets and specialty stores.

YIELD: 6 TO 8 SERVINGS

1/2	cup (1 stick) butter
1	cup wild rice, rinsed and drained
8	ounces mushrooms, sliced
8	ounces water chestnuts, sliced
1/4	cup finely chopped onion
3	chicken bouillon cubes
3	cups hot water

Melt the butter in a large skillet over medium heat. Add the rice, mushrooms, water chestnuts and onion and cook for 30 minutes, stirring occasionally. The rice will turn very dark. Preheat the oven to 325 degrees. Dissolve the bouillon cubes in the water in a 2-quart glass baking dish. Add the rice mixture and mix well. Bake, covered, for 1½ hours, stirring every 30 minutes.

For the best results, do not use long grain and wild rice in place of the wild rice, and do not use canned chicken broth in place of the bouillon cubes and water.

Barley Pilaf with Pine Nuts

YIELD: 6 SERVINGS

1	cup pearl barley
6	tablespoons (3/4 stick) butter
3	ounces (about 1/3 cup) pine nuts
1	cup finely chopped scallions
1/3	cup chopped fresh curly leaf parsley
1/4	teaspoon salt
1/4	teaspoon freshly ground pepper
1 1/3	cups chicken broth

Preheat the oven to 350 degrees. Rinse the barley in cold water and drain. Melt the butter in a skillet over medium-high heat. Add the pine nuts and sauté until light brown. Remove the pine nuts with a slotted spoon to a small bowl. Sauté the scallions and barley in the skillet for 5 to 7 minutes or until the barley is lightly toasted. Remove from the heat. Stir in the pine nuts, parsley, salt and pepper.

Spoon into a 2-quart baking dish. Place the chicken broth in a microwave-safe bowl. Microwave on High for 2 minutes. Pour over the barley mixture and mix well. Bake for 70 minutes or until the broth is absorbed, stirring occasionally. Serve immediately.

Quinoa Mushroom Pilaf

This tiny whole grain is packed with flavor and protein.

YIELD: 8 SERVINGS

1	cup quinoa
2	tablespoons unsalted butter
½	cup finely chopped shallots
1	garlic clove, minced
1	cup chopped cremini mushrooms
2	cups chicken broth
1	tablespoon olive oil
	Salt and freshly ground pepper
1	tablespoon chopped fresh parsley

Place the quinoa in a strainer. Rinse with cold water, rubbing the grains to remove the skins, until the water runs clear. Heat the butter in a large sauté pan over medium heat. Add the shallots, garlic and mushrooms and sauté for 5 to 7 minutes or until the mushrooms are softened.

Increase the heat to medium-high and add the quinoa. Cook for 2 to 3 minutes or until the quinoa is lightly toasted, stirring frequently. Add the chicken broth, olive oil, salt and pepper. Reduce the heat to medium-low and cook, covered, for 12 to 15 minutes or until the quinoa is tender and the liquid is absorbed. Sprinkle with the parsley and serve.

Say keen-wah. That's how you pronounce quinoa—the South American supergrain that's loaded with protein and vital nutrients. It's available packaged as a grain, ground into flour and in several forms of pasta. You can find it in most whole foods stores and some supermarkets.

Risotto with Chicken-Mushroom Medley

This is a quick, easy risotto and serves as a hearty starter or entrée complement.

YIELD: 8 TO 10 SERVINGS

2	tablespoons butter
1	pound boneless skinless chicken breasts, chopped
¼	cup (½ stick) butter
1½	cups long grain rice
1	garlic clove, minced
1	pound assorted mushrooms, such as cremini, button and portobello, sliced
2	shallots, finely chopped
2	cups chicken stock
1	cup white wine
1	cup (4 ounces) freshly grated Parmesan cheese

Melt 2 tablespoons butter in a large skillet over medium heat. Add the chicken and sauté until brown and cooked through. Remove the chicken to a bowl. Add ¼ cup butter, the rice and garlic to the skillet and cook until the rice is light brown, stirring constantly. Add the mushrooms and shallots and mix well. Cook until the mushrooms are soft, stirring frequently.

Stir in the chicken stock and wine. Bring to a boil. Reduce the heat and simmer, covered, for 15 minutes. Add the chicken and simmer for 5 minutes or until the chicken is heated through and the rice is tender. Add the Parmesan cheese and mix well. Serve immediately.

Ginger Fried Rice

(PICTURED ON PAGE 102)

YIELD: 6 SERVINGS

1	egg
1	tablespoon water
1	teaspoon vegetable oil
3	scallions
2	tablespoons vegetable oil
1½	tablespoons minced fresh gingerroot
1	teaspoon kosher salt
4	ounces fresh oyster mushrooms, trimmed and sliced
12	ounces fresh button mushrooms, trimmed and sliced
3	cups cold cooked white rice
1	teaspoon sesame oil

Combine the egg and water in a small bowl and beat until blended. Heat a large nonstick skillet over medium heat. Add ½ teaspoon vegetable oil and swirl to coat the bottom of the skillet. Add half the egg mixture and swirl to form a thin layer over the bottom of the skillet. Cook until the egg is set, forming a thin pancake. Do not stir. Remove with a spatula to a plate to cool. Repeat the procedure with ½ teaspoon vegetable oil and the remaining egg mixture. Roll the pancakes and cut into thin slices.

Chop the scallions, keeping the bulbs and tops separate. Heat 2 tablespoons vegetable oil in a skillet over high heat until the oil begins to smoke. Add the gingerroot, kosher salt and scallion bulbs and cook for 30 seconds, stirring constantly. Add the mushrooms and cook for 4 to 5 minutes or until the mushrooms turn dark and release their liquid. Add the rice and mix well. Cook for 12 to 15 minutes or until the rice is light brown, stirring frequently. Remove from the heat. Add the scallion tops, egg pancake slices and sesame oil and toss gently to combine. Serve immediately.

The root of it.

Good gingerroot has smooth skin and a fresh, spicy fragrance. You can wrap and store unpeeled gingerroot in the refrigerator for up to three weeks, or freeze it for up to six months—slice off a piece of the unthawed root and return the rest to the freezer.

Entrées

Above: Grilled Parmesan Lime Chicken (page 135). Opposite page from top to bottom: Cumin-Dusted Fish Fillets on Green Rice (page 139), Herbed Shrimp with Asparagus (page 143), Habanero Pasta (page 144), Pork Tenderloin with Rosemary (page 132).

Beef Tenderloin with Artichoke Spinach Stuffing

YIELD: 12 TO 14 SERVINGS

10	ounces fresh spinach, trimmed
2	(6-ounce) jars marinated artichoke hearts, drained and chopped
8	ounces crumbled blue cheese
	Freshly ground pepper to taste
1/4	cup dry red wine
1	(5-pound) beef tenderloin
1	cup dry red wine
	Kosher salt to taste

Preheat the oven to 400 degrees. Combine the spinach with 4 to 5 tablespoons water in a non-reactive dish. Microwave, covered, on High until the spinach is wilted; drain and chop the spinach. Combine with the artichoke hearts, blue cheese and pepper in a bowl and mix well. Add 1/4 cup wine and mix well.

Cut a horizontal pocket in the tenderloin, cutting to within 1/2 inch of either end. Spoon the spinach mixture into the pocket. Press the edge to close and secure with wooden skewers.

Place the tenderloin in a shallow baking dish. Pour 1 cup wine over the tenderloin. Sprinkle with kosher salt and pepper. Bake for 20 to 30 minutes for rare or 30 to 40 minutes for medium-rare. Cut into 3/4-inch slices to serve.

Martha's Vineyard Wine Selection:
Rosenblum 2000 Hillside Syrah

Four-season allure.

Charlevoix, Harbor

Springs, Petoskey,

and Traverse City.

West Michigan's

northern coast offers

a plethora of activity

throughout the year.

Spring? Bring on the

golf. Summer? It's all

about resort towns,

boating, and beaches.

Fall is the season for

spectacular views as

the changing trees

display vivid color.

And winter is a

jackpot for outdoor

enthusiasts with skiing,

skating, sledding,

snowmobiling, and

ice fishing.

Fillet of Beef with Herb Crust

3	tablespoons chopped fresh basil
4	large garlic cloves
2	large bay leaves
1	large shallot, quartered
1	tablespoon sea salt
1	teaspoon freshly ground pepper
2	tablespoons olive oil
2	(2-pound) beef tenderloins, trimmed

Process the basil, garlic, bay leaves, shallot, sea salt and pepper in a food processor until finely chopped. Add the olive oil gradually, processing constantly until thickened. Spread the mixture evenly over both tenderloins. Place the tenderloins in a large glass dish. Chill, covered, for 8 hours.

Remove the tenderloins from the refrigerator 30 minutes prior to cooking. Preheat the oven to 400 degrees. Place the tenderloins on a rack in a large roasting pan and insert a meat thermometer.

Roast for 35 to 45 minutes or until the meat thermometer reads 125 degrees for rare to 135 degrees for medium-rare. Remove from the oven and let stand, covered with foil, for 10 minutes. Slice into 8 to 10 pieces and serve.

Martha's Vineyard
Wine Selection:
Franciscan Oakville Estate
2001 Magnificat

Beef Tenderloin Bourguignonne

(PICTURED ON PAGE 124)

YIELD: 8 TO 10 SERVINGS

4	slices thick-cut bacon
3	pounds beef tenderloin, trimmed
	Kosher salt and freshly ground pepper to taste
3	tablespoons olive oil
3	garlic cloves, chopped
1¾	cups burgundy
2	cups beef stock
1½	tablespoons tomato paste
1	small bay leaf
1	large sprig fresh thyme
1	teaspoon chopped fresh rosemary
1	teaspoon kosher salt
½	teaspoon freshly ground pepper
10	carrots, cut on the diagonal into 1-inch pieces
12	ounces red pearl onions
2	tablespoons unsalted butter, softened
2	tablespoons flour
12	ounces mixed mushrooms, such as morel, button or portobello, sliced
1	tablespoon unsalted butter
1	tablespoon olive oil

Fry the bacon in a skillet until crisp-cooked; drain, reserving 2 tablespoons drippings. Crumble the bacon. Cut the tenderloin into 12 pieces. Sprinkle with kosher salt and pepper. Heat 3 tablespoons olive oil in a large skillet over medium-high heat. Sauté the beef in the olive oil until brown on all sides. Remove the beef to a plate.

Heat the reserved bacon drippings in the skillet over medium-high heat. Add the garlic and cook for 30 seconds. Deglaze the skillet with the wine, cooking for 1 minute and scraping the browned bits from the bottom of the skillet. Add the beef stock, tomato paste, bay leaf, thyme, rosemary, 1 teaspoon kosher salt and ½ teaspoon pepper. Bring to a boil over medium-high heat. Boil for 10 minutes, stirring occasionally. Strain the sauce into a bowl, discarding the garlic, bay leaf and thyme. Return the sauce to the skillet and add the carrots and onions and mix well. Reduce the heat and simmer, covered, for 5 minutes.

Simmer, uncovered, for 15 minutes, stirring frequently. Combine 2 tablespoons butter and the flour in a small bowl and mix well. Add to the carrot mixture gradually, stirring constantly. Increase the heat to medium-high and cook for 2 to 3 minutes or until thickened, stirring constantly. Thin with additional beef stock if the mixture becomes too thick.

Sauté the mushrooms in 1 tablespoon butter and 1 tablespoon olive oil in a skillet over medium-high heat for 8 to 10 minutes or until tender. Add the mushrooms and beef to the carrot mixture. Simmer, covered, for 5 to 10 minutes or until heated through.

Remove the beef with a slotted spoon to a serving platter. Arrange the vegetables around the beef and top with the sauce. Garnish with fresh thyme sprigs.

Crispy Orange Beef

This pungent ginger-orange sauce is also a good complement for chicken.

YIELD: 6 SERVINGS

2	pounds flank steak, thinly sliced
1/3	cup sugar
1/2	cup rice wine vinegar
3	tablespoons frozen orange juice concentrate, thawed
1	teaspoon salt
2	tablespoons soy sauce
3	tablespoons minced fresh gingerroot
1 1/2	tablespoons minced garlic
1	tablespoon grated orange zest
1/4	cup cornstarch
	Vegetable oil for frying
	Florets of 1 bunch broccoli, steamed
	Cooked white rice

Pat the beef dry with paper towels. Place in a bowl and chill, covered, for 30 minutes. Combine the sugar, vinegar, orange juice concentrate, salt and soy sauce in a small bowl and whisk until blended. Combine the gingerroot, garlic and orange zest in a small bowl and mix well.

Sprinkle the beef with the cornstarch, turning to coat. Heat 1/4 cup oil in a large heavy skillet over medium-high heat. Fry the meat in batches in the hot oil until crispy and golden brown, scraping the bottom of the skillet and adding additional oil as needed. Remove the meat with a slotted spoon to a bowl and keep warm.

Drain the skillet, reserving 1 tablespoon oil. Cook the gingerroot mixture in the oil over medium-high heat for a few seconds to release the flavor. Add the soy sauce mixture and stir to deglaze the skillet, scraping the browned bits from the bottom of the skillet. Bring the mixture to a boil and boil for 5 minutes or until thickened, stirring frequently. Add the beef and broccoli and stir to coat. Cook until heated through. Remove the beef and broccoli with a slotted spoon to a serving platter. Serve with rice and the sauce from the skillet.

Teriyaki Marinated Steak with Pineapple Salsa

YIELD: 4 TO 6 SERVINGS

Pineapple Salsa

2	tablespoons vegetable oil
1	tablespoon fresh lime juice
1	teaspoon honey
1/2	teaspoon minced fresh gingerroot
	Salt and white pepper to taste
1	cup finely chopped fresh pineapple
1/4	cup finely chopped red bell pepper
2	tablespoons finely chopped white onion
2	teaspoons chopped fresh parsley

Teriyaki Steak

1/3	cup pineapple juice
1/4	cup soy sauce
2	tablespoons chopped white onion
2	tablespoons vegetable oil
2	tablespoons Dijon mustard
1	tablespoon sliced fresh gingerroot
2	tablespoons cider vinegar
1	tablespoon honey
2	to 3 garlic cloves, chopped
1/2	teaspoon thyme
1 1/2	pounds flank steak

For the salsa, combine the oil, lime juice, honey and gingerroot in a small bowl and whisk to mix well. Season with salt and white pepper. Combine the pineapple, bell pepper, onion and parsley in a medium bowl. Add the oil mixture and toss to coat. Let stand for 30 minutes.

For the steak, combine the pineapple juice, soy sauce, onion, oil, mustard, gingerroot, vinegar, honey, garlic and thyme in a bowl and mix well. Pour over the steak in a shallow dish, turning to coat. Marinate, covered, in the refrigerator for 8 hours, turning occasionally.

Remove the steak from the marinade, reserving the marinade. Grill the steak over hot coals for 5 to 7 minutes on each side or until done to taste, basting several times with the reserved marinade. Remove to a serving platter, slice thinly against the grain and serve with the salsa. You may cook the steak in a 375-degree oven if preferred.

Martha's Vineyard Wine Selection:
Leasingham 2001 Magnus Cabernet Sauvignon/Shiraz

Grilled Pork Chops with Dried Cherry Sauce

YIELD: 6 SERVINGS

3	tablespoons balsamic vinegar
3	tablespoons sugar
1	cup dry red wine
1/4	cup minced shallot
1	(3-inch) cinnamon stick
2/3	cup unsalted chicken broth
1	cup dried cherries
1	tablespoon cornstarch
1	tablespoon cold water
2	teaspoons fresh lemon juice
1	tablespoon unsalted butter
	Freshly ground pepper to taste
6	(1-inch-thick) boneless pork chops
	Vegetable oil
	Salt to taste

Bring the vinegar and sugar to a boil in a heavy saucepan over medium heat. Boil for 5 to 7 minutes or until the mixture is of a glaze consistency, stirring frequently. Stir in the wine, shallot and cinnamon stick. Boil for 16 to 18 minutes or until the mixture is reduced to about 1/4 cup, stirring frequently. Add the chicken broth and cherries and cook for 5 minutes or until the cherries plump, stirring frequently. Dissolve the cornstarch in the water in a small bowl. Stir into the cherry sauce 1 teaspoon at a time until the sauce reaches the desired consistency.

Discard the cinnamon stick. Simmer for 2 minutes. Stir in the lemon juice, butter and pepper. Remove from the heat and cover.

Pat the pork chops dry with paper towels. Rub oil lightly over both sides of the pork chops. Season with salt and pepper. Grill over hot coals for 6 to 8 minutes on each side or until cooked through. Remove the pork chops to a serving platter. Spoon the cherry sauce over the pork chops and serve.

Asian Pork Tenderloin

YIELD: 8 TO 10 SERVINGS

1/2	cup soy sauce
1/4	cup tamari sauce
1/4	cup Worcestershire sauce
1/4	cup sake or dry white wine
2	to 3 tablespoons hoisin sauce
2	tablespoons finely chopped gingerroot
2	garlic cloves, pressed
2	tablespoons brown sugar
2	(1 1/2-pound) pork tenderloins
2	tablespoons toasted sesame seeds

Combine the soy sauce, tamari sauce, Worcestershire sauce, sake, hoisin sauce, gingerroot, garlic and brown sugar in a bowl and mix well. Pour over the pork in a large bowl, turning to coat. Chill, covered, for 4 to 24 hours. Remove from the refrigerator 30 minutes prior to cooking.

Preheat the oven to 350 degrees. Drain the marinade and discard. Place the tenderloins in a baking dish and insert a meat thermometer. Bake for 25 to 30 minutes or to 160 degrees on a meat thermometer for medium, or to 170 degrees for well done. Remove from the oven and sprinkle with the sesame seeds. Cover loosely with foil and let stand for 10 minutes. Slice and serve immediately.

Pork Tenderloin with Mushroom-Wine Sauce

YIELD: 4 SERVINGS

1	(1 1/2-pound) pork tenderloin
	Salt and freshly ground pepper to taste
2	tablespoons butter
1	garlic clove, finely chopped
1	cup dry red wine
2	tablespoons tomato paste
8	ounces (about 3 cups) sliced mushrooms
2	tablespoons chopped scallion tops
	Rice pilaf or buttered egg noodles

Cut the tenderloin diagonally into 1/2-inch slices. Sprinkle lightly with salt and pepper. Melt the butter in a large sauté pan over medium heat. Add the garlic and sauté for 1 to 2 minutes or until golden. Add the pork slices and cook for 8 to 10 minutes or until cooked through, turning once. Remove the pork to a plate and cover to keep warm. Increase the heat to medium-high and add the wine. Stir to deglaze the sauté pan, scraping the browned bits from the bottom of the pan. Stir in the tomato paste. Bring the mixture to a boil. Reduce the heat and simmer gently for 3 to 5 minutes or until the mixture is slightly reduced, stirring frequently.

Add the mushrooms and cook for 4 to 6 minutes or until the mushrooms are tender, stirring occasionally. Add the pork and cook for 1 minute or until heated through. Remove to a serving platter. Spoon the sauce over the pork and sprinkle with the scallions. Serve with rice pilaf or buttered egg noodles.

Martha's Vineyard Wine Selection:
Trinchero 2001 Pinot Noir

Pork Tenderloin with Rosemary

(PICTURED ON PAGE 122)

YIELD: 8 TO 10 SERVINGS

2	(1½-pound) pork tenderloins, rolled and tied
¼	cup olive oil
1	tablespoon balsamic vinegar
2	tablespoons chopped fresh rosemary
1½	teaspoons kosher salt
1	tablespoon coarsely ground pepper

Preheat the oven to 350 degrees. Place the tenderloins, marbled side up, in a heavy roasting pan. Roast for 30 minutes. Combine the olive oil, vinegar, rosemary, kosher salt and pepper in a bowl and mix well, crushing the spices with the back of a fork. Remove the pork from the oven and coat evenly with the spice mixture. Insert a meat thermometer.

Roast for 25 to 30 minutes longer or to 155 degrees on a meat thermometer. Remove from the oven and let stand, loosely covered with foil, for 10 minutes. Slice thinly and arrange on a serving platter. Pour the juices from the pan over the slices and serve.

Springtime Lamb Chops

YIELD: 8 SERVINGS

8	lamb rib chops
¼	cup Dijon mustard
2	tablespoons olive oil
2	garlic cloves, minced
¼	cup finely chopped fresh parsley
	Salt and freshly ground pepper to taste

Let the lamb stand at room temperature for 20 minutes. Combine the mustard, olive oil, garlic, parsley, salt and pepper in a small bowl and mix until of a paste consistency. Grill the lamb over medium-hot coals for 5 to 7 minutes or until golden brown. Turn the lamb over.

Spread the mustard mixture evenly over the grilled side of the lamb. Grill, with the cover closed, for 5 to 7 minutes or until the outside is brown but the center is still pink; do not overcook. Serve immediately.

Roasted Rosemary Rack of Lamb with Celery Root Purée

This recipe was provided by Executive Chef David McClimans of the Marigold Lodge.

YIELD: 4 SERVINGS

Celery Root Purée

1	small onion, finely chopped
2	teaspoons butter
2	celery roots, peeled and cut into 1-inch pieces
2	potatoes, peeled and cut into 1-inch pieces
4	cups chicken stock
	Salt and freshly ground pepper to taste

Rack of Lamb

2	French-cut racks of lamb
	Salt and freshly ground pepper to taste
1/4	cup chopped fresh rosemary leaves
1/2	cup olive oil
1	cup dry red wine
1 1/2	cups reduced veal or beef stock
1	teaspoon olive oil
1	bunch fresh asparagus, trimmed and cut lengthwise into thin strips

For the purée, sauté the onion in the butter in a medium saucepan over high heat until translucent. Add the celery roots, potatoes and chicken stock and mix well. Bring to a boil. Reduce the heat and simmer for 10 to 12 minutes or until the celery roots and potatoes are tender, stirring occasionally. Remove from the heat and strain, discarding the liquid. Let the mixture stand until cool. Purée the mixture in a food processor until smooth. Season with salt and pepper. You may prepare the purée up to this point 1 day in advance and chill, covered, in the refrigerator. Reheat the purée before serving, stirring frequently.

For the lamb, preheat the oven to 450 degrees. Cut each lamb rack in half. Season with salt and pepper. Rub evenly with the rosemary. Heat 1/2 cup olive oil in a large skillet over high heat. Add the lamb and sear until brown on each side. Remove from the skillet and place on a baking sheet.

Roast for 10 to 12 minutes or to 120 degrees on a meat thermometer. Remove from the oven and let stand for 5 minutes.

Discard the olive oil from the skillet. Combine the wine and veal stock in the skillet. Simmer over medium heat until reduced by half, stirring occasionally. Season with salt and pepper. Remove from the heat.

Heat 1 teaspoon olive oil in a medium skillet over medium-high heat. Add the asparagus and sauté for 3 to 5 minutes or just until tender. Season the asparagus with salt and pepper.

Arrange the asparagus on the center of a serving platter or on individual plates. Spoon the purée over the asparagus. Cut each lamb rack in half. Stand each rack upright over the purée, crossing the rib bones together. Spoon the stock reduction over the lamb. Garnish with rosemary sprigs and serve.

Martha's Vineyard Wine Selection:
Taurino 1997 Notopanaro

Pretty? No. Delicious? Yes!

Celery root is a whitish, bulbous, baseball-size vegetable with root-like stalks. It's similar in flavor to celery, but it's a different vegetable altogether—one that often gets overlooked because it's so ugly!

Chicken with Lemon and Artichokes

This recipe was provided by Executive Chef Tom Webb of the B.O.B.

YIELD: 4 SERVINGS

2	eggs, lightly beaten
1/4	cup milk
1/2	cup bread crumbs
1/2	cup (2 ounces) grated Parmesan cheese
4	(6-ounce) boneless skinless chicken breasts
	Flour
1/4	cup olive oil
1	shallot, minced
10	ounces artichoke hearts, quartered
	Juice of 1 lemon
1/3	cup white wine
1	tablespoon minced fresh basil
1/2	cup (1 stick) butter
	Salt and freshly ground pepper to taste

Preheat the oven to 300 degrees. Combine the eggs and milk in a shallow dish and whisk until blended. Combine the bread crumbs and Parmesan cheese in a shallow dish. Coat the chicken with flour. Dip in the egg mixture and coat with the Parmesan cheese mixture. Heat a large heavy skillet over medium-high heat. Add the olive oil. Sauté the chicken in the olive oil until golden brown on each side. Remove to a baking pan. Bake for 20 minutes.

Drain the skillet, reserving 1 tablespoon of the olive oil. Sauté the shallot in the olive oil over medium-high heat until tender.

Add the artichoke hearts, lemon juice and wine and cook until the liquid is reduced by half, stirring occasionally. Add the basil and butter and heat until the butter melts, swirling the pan to create a smooth sauce. Season with salt and pepper. Arrange the chicken on a serving platter. Pour the sauce over the chicken and serve.

Martha's Vineyard Wine Selection:
Far Niente 2001 Chardonnay

Grilled Parmesan Lime Chicken

(PICTURED ON PAGE 123)

Perfect for a summertime cookout, this dish is also terrific when substituting fish or shrimp for the chicken.

YIELD: 4 TO 6 SERVINGS

Parmesan Lime Sauce

2	tablespoons fresh lime juice
1	teaspoon anchovy paste (optional)
3	garlic cloves, minced
1/2	cup (2 ounces) freshly grated Parmesan cheese
1/3	cup olive oil
	Kosher salt and freshly ground pepper to taste

Lime Chicken

1/3	cup extra-virgin olive oil
1/3	cup bottled Key lime juice
1/2	to 1 teaspoon hot pepper sauce, or to taste
2	tablespoons chopped mixed fresh herbs, such as cilantro, chives and parsley
6	boneless skinless chicken breasts

For the sauce, combine the lime juice, anchovy paste, garlic and Parmesan cheese in a small bowl and mix well. Add the olive oil gradually, whisking constantly. Season with kosher salt and pepper. Let stand for 30 minutes. Whisk just before serving. This may be prepared up to 1 day in advance. Chill, covered, in the refrigerator. Bring to room temperature and whisk before serving.

For the chicken, combine the olive oil, Key lime juice, hot pepper sauce and herbs in a large sealable plastic bag. Add the chicken, turning to coat well. Marinate in the refrigerator for 3 to 8 hours. Drain the chicken, discarding the marinade. Grill over medium-hot coals for 5 to 7 minutes on each side or until cooked through. Serve with the sauce and garnish with lime wedges. If substituting fish or shrimp for the chicken, marinate for no longer than 30 minutes.

Cheese-Stuffed Chicken Breasts in Phyllo

This entrée is easily multiplied for large groups and may be made a day ahead of serving. Refrigerate until ready to bake.

YIELD: 8 SERVINGS

Cheese Stuffing

1½	cups (6 ounces) shredded sharp Cheddar cheese
1½	cups (6 ounces) shredded Monterey Jack cheese
1	teaspoon freshly ground pepper
1	teaspoon tarragon
1	cup chopped fresh parsley
¼	cup (½ stick) butter, softened

Chicken

8	boneless skinless chicken breasts
8	sheets phyllo, cut into halves crosswise
½	to 1 cup (1 to 2 sticks) butter, melted

For the stuffing, combine the cheeses, pepper, tarragon, parsley and ¼ cup butter in a bowl and mix well.

For the chicken, preheat the oven to 350 degrees. Cover the phyllo with a clean, damp kitchen towel. Place the chicken between 2 pieces of waxed paper and flatten to ½ inch with a meat mallet. Lay 1 sheet of phyllo on a work surface and brush with butter. Layer with a second sheet of phyllo and brush with butter. Place a chicken breast along the short edge of the phyllo, leaving a border on either side.

Spread ⅛ of the stuffing over the chicken breast. Roll to enclose the filling, tucking in the sides after 1 roll. Repeat the procedure with the remaining phyllo, chicken and stuffing. Brush the phyllo packets with butter. Arrange in a single layer seam side down in a 9x13-inch baking dish. Bake for 40 minutes or until the phyllo is golden brown. Serve immediately.

Martha's Vineyard Wine Selection:
Ferrari Carano 2001 Fume Blanc

Mediterranean Chicken

YIELD: 4 SERVINGS

1	tablespoon olive oil
1/4	cup chopped white onion
2	garlic cloves, crushed
1	pound boneless skinless chicken breasts
1/3	cup red wine vinegar
4	plum tomatoes, seeded and chopped (about 2 cups)
1	teaspoon chopped fresh thyme
1/2	teaspoon salt
1/4	teaspoon freshly ground pepper
	Hot cooked white rice

Heat the olive oil in a skillet over medium-high heat. Add the onion and garlic and sauté for 2 to 3 minutes. Cut the chicken across the grain into 1/2-inch slices. Add the chicken to the skillet. Cook for 5 minutes or until the chicken is cooked through, stirring frequently. Stir in the vinegar, tomatoes, thyme, salt and pepper. Bring the mixture to a boil.

Reduce the heat and simmer gently for 5 minutes or until the liquid is slightly reduced, stirring occasionally. Serve over rice.

Martha's Vineyard Wine Selection:
Terra D'Oro 2001 Sangiovese

Spicy Chicken Pizza

YIELD: 4 SERVINGS

1/2	cup rice vinegar
1/4	cup soy sauce
3	tablespoons water
1/4	cup packed brown sugar
4	garlic cloves, minced
1	tablespoon minced gingerroot
1/2	teaspoon red pepper flakes
2	tablespoons peanut butter
8	ounces boneless chicken breasts, cut into bite-size pieces
1	tablespoon olive oil
3/4	cup (3 ounces) shredded mozzarella cheese
1	baked (12-inch) thin pizza crust
1/2	cup chopped scallions

Combine the vinegar, soy sauce, water, brown sugar, garlic, gingerroot, red pepper and peanut butter in a small bowl and mix well. Sauté the chicken in the olive oil in a skillet for 3 minutes or until cooked through. Remove the chicken to a plate. Add the peanut butter mixture to the skillet. Bring to a boil over medium-high heat. Cook for 5 to 7 minutes or until thickened, stirring frequently. Add the chicken and cook for 1 minute longer.

Preheat the oven to 450 degrees. Sprinkle the cheese on the pizza crust. Top with the chicken mixture. Place the pizza directly on the oven rack. Bake for 10 minutes or until the cheese is melted and the topping is bubbly. Remove from the oven and let stand for 5 minutes. Sprinkle with the scallions, cut into wedges and serve.

Sesame Noodle Chicken with Tri-Colored Peppers

YIELD: 4 SERVINGS

2	tablespoons sesame oil
1/4	teaspoon red pepper
1/3	cup creamy peanut butter
3	tablespoons soy sauce
2	tablespoons dry sherry
1	tablespoon vinegar
2	tablespoons water
2	teaspoons sugar
1	pound boneless skinless chicken breasts, cut into 1/2-inch strips
8	ounces uncooked vermicelli
1/4	cup plus 1 tablespoon vegetable oil
8	ounces mushrooms, quartered
1	small red bell pepper, cut into thin strips
1	small yellow bell pepper, cut into thin strips
1	small orange bell pepper, cut into thin strips
1	bunch green onions, cut into 1-inch pieces
1/2	teaspoon salt
1	teaspoon sesame seeds

Heat the sesame oil in a small pan over medium heat. Add the red pepper and cook for 1 minute, stirring frequently. Add the peanut butter, soy sauce, sherry, vinegar, water and sugar and mix well. Cook until the sauce is smooth, stirring frequently. Remove from the heat. Place the chicken in a bowl. Coat with 1/4 of the peanut butter mixture.

Cook the vermicelli al dente using the package directions; drain. Combine the pasta and 1 tablespoon vegetable oil in a saucepan and toss to coat. Cover the saucepan to keep the pasta warm.

Heat 1/4 cup vegetable oil in a large skillet or wok over high heat. Add the mushrooms, bell peppers, green onions, salt and chicken strips. Cook for 5 minutes or until the vegetables are tender-crisp and the chicken is cooked through, stirring frequently. Add the chicken mixture and the remaining peanut butter mixture to the pasta and toss to combine. Spoon onto a serving platter. Sprinkle with the sesame seeds and serve.

Cumin-Dusted Fish Fillets on Green Rice

(PICTURED ON PAGE 122)

This dish is fantastic with a variety of firm white fish, such as swordfish, sea bass, and halibut.

YIELD: 4 SERVINGS

Wine Sauce

1	egg yolk, lightly beaten
1/3	cup dry white wine
1/3	cup chicken broth
1/4	cup fresh lime juice
2	tablespoons honey
1	teaspoon cornstarch

Green Rice

1 1/4	cups water
1	tablespoon fresh lime juice
1/2	cup uncooked long grain rice
3/4	cup chopped onion
2	garlic cloves, minced
1	bay leaf
1/2	teaspoon kosher salt
	Freshly ground pepper to taste
1	tablespoon chopped fresh cilantro
1	tablespoon chopped fresh flat-leaf parsley

Fish Fillets

2	(1-inch-thick) firm white fish fillets
2	teaspoons cumin
	Salt and freshly ground pepper to taste
1	teaspoon olive oil

For the sauce, whisk together the egg yolk, wine, chicken broth, lime juice, honey and cornstarch in a small saucepan. Simmer for 4 to 5 minutes or until slightly thickened, whisking constantly. Remove from the heat.

For the rice, bring the water and lime juice to a boil in a 2-quart saucepan. Add the rice, onion, garlic, bay leaf, kosher salt and pepper and mix well. Bring to a boil. Reduce the heat to low and cook, covered, for 15 to 17 minutes or until the rice is tender and the liquid is absorbed. Fluff the rice with a fork and let stand, covered, for 5 minutes. Stir in the cilantro and parsley.

For the fish, preheat the oven to 500 degrees. Rinse the fish and pat dry. Sprinkle both sides with the cumin, salt and pepper. Heat the olive oil in a 10-inch cast-iron skillet over high heat. Add the fish and sear for 5 minutes or until browned. Turn the fish over and place the skillet on the upper rack in the oven. Bake for 6 to 8 minutes or just until cooked through. Remove from the oven and cut the fish into halves crosswise. Mound the rice on a serving platter. Arrange the fish in the center of the platter. Spoon the sauce over and around the fish and serve.

Fish stories.

Whether it's the first bluegill pulled out of a pond by a toddler, a proud salmon sweated into submission on Lake Michigan, or a glistening trout won with a hand-tied fly, we Michiganders love our fish. Tip: Thaw frozen fish in milk to eliminate that "freezer taste."

Pan-Crisped Lake Fish with Lemon Dijon Sauce

YIELD: 4 TO 6 SERVINGS

Lemon Dijon Sauce

1	cup mayonnaise
2	teaspoons fresh lemon juice
1	teaspoon Dijon mustard
1/2	teaspoon Worcestershire sauce
1/4	teaspoon hot pepper sauce
1	tablespoon capers
1/2	teaspoon tarragon
1/4	cup finely chopped dill pickle
2	tablespoons minced onion
1	tablespoon chopped fresh parsley
	Kosher salt and freshly ground pepper to taste

Fish

1/2	cup milk
1	teaspoon maple syrup
1 1/2 to 2	pounds white freshwater fish fillets
30	saltine crackers
1/2	cup dried potato flakes
	Dash of cayenne pepper
2	eggs
2	tablespoons milk
3	tablespoons vegetable oil

For the sauce, combine the mayonnaise, lemon juice, mustard, Worcestershire sauce, hot pepper sauce, capers and tarragon in a blender and process until blended. Spoon into a bowl. Add the pickle, onion, parsley, kosher salt and pepper and mix well. Chill, covered, for 1 hour to 2 days.

For the fish, combine 1/2 cup milk and the syrup in a shallow dish and mix well. Place the fish in the milk mixture and let stand for 20 to 30 minutes, turning occasionally.

Combine the crackers, potato flakes and cayenne pepper in a food processor and pulse until crushed. Pour into a shallow dish. Combine the eggs and 2 tablespoons milk in a shallow dish and whisk until blended. Remove the fish from the milk mixture, shaking off the excess liquid. Dip the fillets in the egg mixture. Coat with the cracker mixture. Heat the oil in a large heavy skillet over medium-high heat. Add the fish and sauté for 4 to 6 minutes on each side or until the fish flakes easily with a fork. Serve with the sauce.

Caramelized Salmon with Cilantro Potato Salad

This dish is the creation of Chef Joe Pagano, owner of Raffaela's by Pagano's.

YIELD: 8 SERVINGS

Fresh Lemon Mayonnaise

1	pasteurized egg
1	tablespoon Dijon mustard
2	tablespoons fresh lemon juice
2	cups olive oil
	Salt and freshly ground pepper to taste

Potato Salad

1	pound new potatoes or small red potatoes, quartered
1/4	cup chopped fresh cilantro
1	teaspoon chopped garlic
1/3	cup finely chopped red onion
1/3	cup finely chopped celery
	Salt and freshly ground pepper to taste

Salmon

4	(4-ounce) salmon fillets, cut into halves crosswise
	Kosher salt and freshly ground pepper to taste
1	cup sugar
2	tablespoons olive oil

For the mayonnaise, process the egg, mustard and lemon juice in a food processor for 20 seconds. Add the olive oil gradually, processing at high speed constantly until the mixture thickens. Season with salt and pepper and blend by pulsing 1 or 2 times. Chill, in an airtight container, for up to 24 hours.

For the potato salad, combine the potatoes with enough salted water to cover in a large saucepan. Bring to a boil and cook until the potatoes are tender; drain. Let stand until cool. Combine 1 cup of the mayonnaise, the cilantro, garlic, onion and celery in a large bowl and mix well. Season with salt and pepper. Add the potatoes and stir gently to combine. Season with additional salt and pepper. Chill, covered, for 1 hour. Reserve the remaining mayonnaise for another use—it is best if used within 24 hours.

For the salmon, season each salmon fillet with kosher salt and pepper. Coat with the sugar, tapping the fillets to remove any excess sugar. Heat the olive oil in a large skillet over medium-high heat. Add the salmon and sauté for 2 to 3 minutes on each side or until the sugar caramelizes. Spoon the potato salad onto the center of a serving platter. Arrange the fillets around the potato salad. Garnish with sprigs of cilantro and curly leaf parsley and serve immediately.

Martha's Vineyard Wine Selection:
Rombauer 2002 Chardonnay Carneros

Fish CAN climb ladders.

Just ask David Letterman. Built along the Grand River to aid spawning fish in their struggle to swim upstream, the Fish Ladder gained national attention when the late-night television host selected Grand Rapids as his fictional "home office"— largely because he was fascinated with the Fish Ladder!

Shrimp and Chicken Au Gratin

YIELD: 6 SERVINGS

3/4	cup milk
1/4	cup flour
1/2	teaspoon white pepper
1/2	cup (2 ounces) shredded sharp Cheddar cheese
2/3	cup Champagne or white wine
1/4	cup (1/2 stick) butter
8	ounces mushrooms, sliced
2	tablespoons minced shallots
2	tablespoons butter
1/2	cup fresh plain bread crumbs
4	boneless skinless chicken breasts, cooked and chopped
1	pound medium shrimp, peeled, deveined and cooked
2	(10-ounce) packages frozen artichoke hearts, cooked, drained and quartered
2	cups (8 ounces) shredded sharp Cheddar cheese

Whisk together the milk, flour and white pepper in a large saucepan. Bring to a boil over medium-high heat, stirring constantly. Remove from the heat and stir in 1/2 cup cheese. Stir until the cheese is melted. Stir in the Champagne. Cover and keep warm.

Preheat the oven to 375 degrees. Melt 1/4 cup butter in a large skillet over medium-high heat. Add the mushrooms and shallots and sauté for 5 minutes or until the shallots are tender. Remove from the heat. Melt 2 tablespoons butter in a small skillet over medium-high heat. Add the bread crumbs and cook until lightly toasted, stirring frequently.

Combine the cheese sauce, mushroom mixture, chicken, shrimp, artichokes and 2 cups cheese in a large bowl. Spoon into a buttered 2-quart baking dish. Top with the bread crumbs. Bake for 30 minutes or until golden brown and bubbling around the edges. Serve hot.

Herbed Shrimp with Asparagus

(PICTURED ON PAGE 122)

Elegant, beautiful, and easy to prepare, this is a perfect dish for an intimate dinner at home.

YIELD: 4 SERVINGS

24	stalks asparagus, peeled and trimmed
1/3	cup olive oil
2	small garlic cloves, minced
2	teaspoons chopped shallot
24	large shrimp, peeled and deveined
1/4	cup flour
1/2	cup dry white wine
2	tablespoons chopped fresh parsley
2	tablespoons chopped chives
2	tablespoons chopped fresh basil
1 1/2	teaspoons chopped fresh thyme
	Salt and freshly ground pepper to taste
2	cups finely chopped seeded tomatoes
1/4	cup (1/2 stick) chilled butter
2	tablespoons butter, melted

Steam the asparagus over boiling water until tender-crisp; drain. Let stand, covered. Heat the olive oil in a large skillet over medium-high heat. Add the garlic and shallot and sauté for 2 minutes. Dust the shrimp with the flour. Add the shrimp to the skillet and sauté for 2 minutes. Add the wine, parsley, chives, basil, thyme, salt and pepper and mix well. Simmer for 2 minutes, stirring occasionally. Add the tomatoes and 1/4 cup butter. Cook just until the tomatoes begin to soften and the butter melts, stirring frequently.

Arrange the asparagus on plates. Brush the asparagus tips with the melted butter. Spoon the shrimp mixture over the asparagus. Garnish with basil leaves and serve.

Martha's Vineyard Wine Selection:
Nicolas Feuillate Premier Brut Champagne

Shrimp with Tarragon and Lemon

YIELD: 4 TO 6 SERVINGS

½	cup (1 stick) butter
2	pounds large shrimp, peeled and deveined
½	cup chicken broth
1	tablespoon chopped fresh flat-leaf parsley
½	teaspoon tarragon
1	garlic clove, minced
2	tablespoons lemon juice
2	tablespoons dry sherry
	Cooked white, brown or wild rice

Melt the butter in a large skillet over medium heat. Add the shrimp and sauté for 5 minutes, turning occasionally. Remove the shrimp to a dish and cover to keep warm. Combine the chicken broth, parsley, tarragon, garlic and lemon juice in the skillet. Cook over medium heat for 15 minutes or until the sauce is reduced, stirring frequently.

Add the shrimp and cook for 3 minutes or until heated through, stirring occasionally; do not overcook. Stir in the sherry and remove from the heat. Serve immediately over a bed of rice.

Martha's Vineyard Wine Selection:
Livio Felluga Pinot Grigio 2002

Habanero Pasta

(PICTURED ON THE COVER AND PAGE 122)

Take care to wear gloves when removing seeds from the habanero chile.

YIELD: 6 SERVINGS

6	tablespoons (¾ stick) butter
6	shallots, finely chopped
1	small habanero chile, seeded and minced
2	cups dry white wine
2	(15-ounce) cans diced tomatoes
½	cup chopped fresh basil
1	teaspoon kosher salt
1	pound uncooked penne
	Freshly grated Parmesan cheese

Melt the butter in a medium skillet over medium-high heat. Add the shallots and chile and cook for 4 to 5 minutes or until the shallots are tender. Add the wine, undrained tomatoes, basil and kosher salt and mix well. Simmer gently for 8 to 10 minutes or until slightly reduced, stirring occasionally.

Cook the pasta al dente, using the package directions; drain. Spoon the pasta into a serving bowl. Spoon the tomato sauce over the pasta. Sprinkle with Parmesan cheese and serve.

Linguini with White Clam Sauce

YIELD: 4 SERVINGS

1	cup water
1	cup white wine
3	garlic cloves, chopped
2	pounds fresh clams in the shell, soaked and scrubbed
2	tablespoons unsalted butter
2	tablespoons olive oil
2	cups sliced mushrooms
1	cup chopped shallots
4	garlic cloves, minced
1/8	teaspoon red pepper flakes
1/4	cup flour
2/3	cup dry white wine
2	teaspoons fresh lemon juice
2	cups bottled clam juice
2	(10-ounce) cans whole baby clams
1/2	cup minced fresh flat-leaf parsley
1	tablespoon minced fresh thyme
	Salt and white pepper to taste
1	pound linguini, cooked and drained

Combine the water, 1 cup wine and 3 garlic cloves in a pot fitted with a steamer basket and bring to a boil. Put the fresh clams in the steamer basket. Steam, covered, for 5 minutes or just until the shells begin to open.

Melt the butter in a deep skillet over medium heat. Stir in the olive oil. Add the mushrooms, shallots, 4 garlic cloves and red pepper flakes and sauté until the shallots are golden brown, stirring frequently.

Stir in the flour and cook for 1 minute, stirring constantly. Stir in 2/3 cup wine, the lemon juice, clam juice and undrained clams. Simmer for 5 minutes, stirring frequently. Stir in the parsley, thyme, salt and white pepper. Combine with the steamed clams and pasta in a large serving bowl and toss to mix well. Garnish with lemon wedges and parsley sprigs and serve.

Turkey Tettrazini with Spinach Fettuccini

12	ounces uncooked spinach fettuccini, broken into pieces
1/4	cup (1/2 stick) butter
8	ounces button mushrooms, trimmed and sliced
1	large yellow onion, coarsely chopped
3	tablespoons flour
1	teaspoon salt
1	teaspoon garlic pepper blend
	Dash of cayenne pepper
	Dash of hot pepper sauce
1 1/2	cups skim milk
2	cups chopped cooked turkey
1/2	cup (2 ounces) freshly grated Parmesan cheese
1/2	cup white wine, such as Chardonnay or pinot grigio

Cook the pasta in boiling salted water to cover using the package directions; drain. Preheat the oven to 400 degrees. Melt the butter in a large deep skillet over medium-high heat. Add the mushrooms and onion and sauté for 8 minutes or until the onions are translucent and the mushrooms have released their juices. Add the flour, salt, garlic pepper, cayenne pepper and hot pepper sauce. Cook for 2 minutes, stirring constantly. Stir in the milk gradually. Cook for 5 to 10 minutes or until the mixture is thickened and bubbly, stirring constantly. Remove from the heat and stir in the turkey.

Layer half the pasta in a greased 9x13-inch baking pan. Top with half the turkey mixture. Sprinkle with 1/4 cup of the Parmesan cheese and 1/4 cup of the wine. Repeat the layers. Bake for 15 to 20 minutes or until bubbly and the edges begin to brown. Remove from the oven and let stand for 5 minutes before serving.

Farm Stand Pasta

YIELD: 4 SERVINGS

2	tablespoons olive oil
2	teaspoons minced garlic
1	cup (1-inch) asparagus pieces
1	cup broccoli florets
1	cup sliced mushrooms
2/3	cup thinly sliced carrots
1	cup pea pods
2	tablespoons finely chopped fresh parsley
1	tablespoon chopped fresh basil
1/2	to 1 teaspoon salt
1/2	to 1 teaspoon freshly ground pepper
2/3	cup chopped cashews
1 1/4	cups chicken broth or vegetable broth
2	teaspoons cornstarch
8	ounces penne, cooked and drained
1/2	cup (2 ounces) shredded Parmesan cheese

Heat the olive oil in a wok or large skillet over medium-high heat. Add the garlic and sauté for 20 seconds, stirring constantly. Add the asparagus, broccoli, mushrooms and carrots. Cook for 3 minutes, stirring frequently. Add the pea pods, parsley, basil, salt, pepper and cashews. Cook for 1 to 2 minutes or until the vegetables are tender-crisp, stirring frequently.

Whisk together the chicken broth and cornstarch in a small bowl. Pour over the vegetables. Cook until the sauce is thickened and bubbly, stirring constantly. Add the pasta and toss to combine. Spoon into a serving bowl. Sprinkle with the Parmesan cheese and serve.

Michigan boasts!

Michigan is the number-one state in boat registrations. The first state to guarantee every child the right to tax-paid high school education. The only state to touch four of the five Great Lakes. Home to one of the world's longest suspension bridges, the Mackinac Bridge. The world's leading producer of dogsleds. Blanketed by more than 19 million acres of forest. The first state to install roadside picnic tables.

Penne with Tomatoes and Olives

Freezing the Havarti cheese for 30 minutes prior to use will make grating much easier.

YIELD: 4 TO 6 SERVINGS

3	tablespoons olive oil
1½	cups chopped onions
2	large garlic cloves, minced
3	(28-ounce) cans whole Italian plum tomatoes
2	teaspoons dried basil
1	teaspoon sugar
1	to 2 teaspoons red pepper flakes
2	cups chicken stock
	Kosher salt and freshly ground black pepper to taste
1	pound uncooked penne
2	tablespoons olive oil
2½	cups (10 ounces) grated Havarti cheese
½	cup sliced kalamata olives
⅓	cup freshly grated Parmesan cheese
⅓	cup finely chopped fresh basil

Heat 3 tablespoons olive oil in a Dutch oven over medium-high heat. Add the onions and garlic and sauté for 5 minutes or until the onions are tender. Add the undrained tomatoes, dried basil, sugar and red pepper and mix well, crushing the tomatoes lightly with the back of a spoon. Bring to a boil, stirring occasionally. Stir in the chicken stock. Bring to a boil. Reduce the heat to medium and simmer for 60 to 70 minutes or until the mixture is thickened, stirring occasionally. Thin with additional stock if necessary. The sauce should yield about 6 cups. Season with kosher salt and black pepper. You may prepare to this point and store, covered, in the refrigerator for up to 2 days.

Preheat the oven to 350 degrees. Cook the pasta al dente, using the package directions; drain. Toss with 2 tablespoons olive oil. Pour the tomato sauce over the pasta and mix well. Stir in the havarti cheese and olives. Spoon into a non-reactive 4-quart baking dish. Sprinkle with the Parmesan cheese. Bake, covered, for 20 minutes. Remove the cover and bake for 10 minutes longer. Sprinkle with the fresh basil and serve.

Martha's Vineyard Wine Selection:
Chapoutier 2000 Bellaruche

Ragù Bolognese with Toasted Noodles

YIELD: 8 SERVINGS

Ragù

1/3	cup olive oil
1 3/4	cups chopped onions
2	slices bacon, finely chopped
2	ounces prosciutto, finely chopped
3	tablespoons chopped garlic
1	pound ground chuck
1	pound ground veal
8	ounces button mushrooms, trimmed and sliced
1/2	cup dry red wine
1/2	ounce dried Italian mushrooms, broken into small pieces
3	tablespoons chopped fresh sage leaves
3 1/2	cups beef broth
1	(6-ounce) can tomato paste
1	(28-ounce) can diced tomatoes

Toasted Noodles

3	cups flour
1	teaspoon salt
1/4	teaspoon freshly ground pepper
1/8	teaspoon freshly grated nutmeg
4	egg yolks
1	egg
1 3/4	cups milk
2	tablespoons olive oil
1/4	cup (1/2 stick) unsalted butter

For the ragù, heat the olive oil in a large heavy saucepan over medium heat. Add the onions, bacon, prosciutto and garlic and sauté for 10 minutes or until the mixture begins to brown. Add the ground chuck and ground veal. Cook until the meat is brown and crumbly, stirring constantly; drain. Add the button mushrooms and cook for 5 minutes or until the juices are released, stirring frequently. Add the wine, dried mushrooms and sage and mix well. Simmer for 4 minutes or until most of the liquid is absorbed, stirring occasionally. Add the beef broth, 1/2 cup at a time, simmering until the liquid is absorbed before adding additional broth. Add the tomato paste and undrained tomatoes and mix well. Simmer for 1 1/2 hours, stirring occasionally and adding water 1/2 cup at a time if necessary to maintain a medium-thick consistency. Remove from the heat. You may prepare the sauce up to 4 days in advance and store, covered, in the refrigerator.

For the noodles, combine the flour, salt, pepper and nutmeg in a medium bowl. Combine the egg yolks, egg and milk in a small bowl and beat until blended. Add to the dry mixture and mix by hand just until blended. Chill, covered, for 30 minutes to 1 hour.

Bring salted water to a boil in a large saucepan. Press the chilled dough through a colander with large holes into the water using the back of a metal spoon. Cook for 4 to 5 minutes or until al dente; drain. Rinse the noodles with cool water. Add the olive oil and mix well.

Melt the butter in a large skillet over high heat, swirling to coat the bottom of the skillet. Add the noodles and sauté until golden brown, stirring constantly. Spoon the ragu into shallow bowls. Top with the noodles and serve.

Above: Pumpkin Cream Roll (page 156). Opposite page from top to bottom: Raspberry Coconut Cake (page 154), Peaches and Cream Pie (page 160), Deep-Dish Strawberry Cream Pie (page 161), Tiramisu Toffee Trifle Pie (page 162), Berries and Mint with a Splash (page 172).

Apple Cake with Caramel Sauce

If you are in search of a new signature "comfort" dessert. . .this is it!

YIELD: 12 SERVINGS

Apple Cake

3	cups flour
2	teaspoons cinnamon
1	teaspoon baking soda
1	teaspoon salt
1	pound apples, peeled and cut into 1/3-inch pieces
1	cup sugar
1	cup packed brown sugar
1 1/2	cups vegetable oil
3	eggs
3	teaspoons vanilla extract
3/4	cup chopped pecans

Caramel Sauce

1/2	cup (1 stick) butter
1	cup packed brown sugar
1/4	cup milk
1	teaspoon vanilla extract

For the cake, preheat the oven to 350 degrees. Sift the flour, cinnamon, baking soda and salt into a medium bowl. Spray a 12-cup bundt pan with nonstick cooking spray. Spoon 3 tablespoons of the flour mixture into the pan, tilting to coat the pan evenly. Combine the apples and 2 tablespoons of the flour mixture in a bowl and toss to coat. Combine the sugar, brown sugar, oil, eggs and vanilla in a mixing bowl and beat until thickened. Beat in the remaining flour mixture gradually. Fold in the apples and pecans. Spoon into the prepared bundt pan.

Bake for 60 minutes or until a cake tester inserted in the center comes out clean. Remove the pan to a wire rack.

For the sauce, melt the butter in a heavy skillet over medium heat. Whisk in the brown sugar and milk. Bring to a boil, whisking constantly until the mixture is smooth. Whisk in the vanilla.

Spoon 1/4 cup of the hot sauce over the warm cake. Let stand for 15 minutes or until the sauce is absorbed. Invert the cake onto a serving plate. Spoon the remaining sauce over the cake. Let stand for 1 hour before serving.

How do you like them apples?

Michigan produces more apples than all other fruits combined— nearly one billion pounds per year. Many are great for pies, including Jonathan, Northern Spy, Golden Delicious, Rome, and Ida Red.

Raspberry Coconut Cake

(PICTURED ON PAGE 150)

This moist and flavor-rich cake makes for a spectacular presentation!

YIELD: 12 TO 16 SERVINGS

Coconut Cake

1	(2-layer) package white cake mix
1¼	cups unsweetened coconut milk
3	eggs
½	cup (1 stick) butter, softened

Pastry Crème

¼	cup milk
½	cup heavy cream
2	egg yolks
¼	cup sugar
1½	tablespoons cornstarch
¼	cup milk
½	teaspoon vanilla extract

Fluffy White Icing

1½	cups sugar
¼	teaspoon cream of tartar
⅛	teaspoon salt
2	egg whites
¼	cup water
½	cup flaked sweetened coconut, toasted

Assembly

1½	cups seedless raspberry jam
½	cup flaked sweetened coconut, toasted

For the cake, preheat the oven using the cake mix package directions. Combine the cake mix, coconut milk, eggs and butter in a large mixing bowl and beat at low speed for 30 seconds. Beat at high speed for 2 minutes, scraping the bowl occasionally. Pour into 2 greased and floured 8-inch round cake pans. Bake using the package directions. Remove to a wire rack to cool.

For the crème, combine ¼ cup milk and the heavy cream in a saucepan over medium-high heat. Bring to a boil, stirring frequently. Remove from the heat. Combine the egg yolks and sugar in a mixing bowl and beat for 2 minutes or until pale yellow. Stir in the cornstarch. Add ¼ cup milk and beat until blended. Add the egg mixture to the milk mixture gradually, whisking constantly. Bring to a boil over medium-high heat, whisking constantly until thickened. Remove from the heat and stir in the vanilla. Let stand until cool.

For the icing, combine the sugar, cream of tartar, salt, egg whites and water in the top of a double boiler over simmering water. Beat at high speed for 5 to 7 minutes or until the sugar is dissolved and soft peaks form. Remove from the heat. Beat until the icing is glossy and of spreading consistency. Stir in the coconut.

To assemble, cut both cakes into halves horizontally. Place 1 cake half, cut side up, on a cake plate. Spread with ½ cup of the jam and ⅓ of the pastry crème. Top with a cake half, cut side down. Spread with ½ cup of the jam and ⅓ of the pastry crème. Repeat the layers with the remaining cake halves, jam and pastry crème, ending with cake. Spread the icing over the top and side of the cake. Sprinkle with the coconut and serve. Keep the cake covered tightly in a cool place if not serving immediately.

Chocolate Zucchini Cake

YIELD: 12 SERVINGS

½	cup (1 stick) butter, softened
1¾	cups sugar
½	cup vegetable oil
2	eggs
1	teaspoon vanilla extract
½	cup sour cream
2½	cups flour
¼	cup cocoa powder
1	teaspoon baking soda
½	teaspoon cinnamon
½	teaspoon salt
2	cups shredded peeled zucchini
½	cup semisweet chocolate chips
	Whipped cream

Preheat the oven to 325 degrees. Cream the butter in a mixing bowl until light and fluffy. Add the sugar and oil and beat until blended. Beat in the eggs, vanilla and sour cream. Combine the flour, cocoa powder, baking soda, cinnamon and salt in a bowl. Add to the creamed mixture and mix well. Stir in the zucchini and chocolate chips.

Pour into a greased 9x13-inch baking pan. Bake for 40 to 50 minutes or until the center springs back when touched. Remove to a wire rack to cool. Slice into squares and serve each square with a dollop of whipped cream.

Spotlight: Noogieland

Hosted by Gilda's Club of West Michigan, Noogieland is a place where children who have cancer—or whose loved ones have cancer—can learn, listen, and laugh. Programs include family nights, SUPER Saturdays, and parties for every special occasion.

Pumpkin Cream Roll

(PICTURED ON PAGE 151)

YIELD: 10 SERVINGS

Pumpkin Cake

3	eggs
1	cup sugar
2/3	cup canned pumpkin
1	teaspoon baking soda
1	teaspoon salt
1/2	teaspoon cinnamon
3/4	cup flour
	Confectioners' sugar

Cream Filling

2	cups confectioners' sugar
3	tablespoons butter, softened
8	ounces cream cheese, softened
1	teaspoon vanilla extract
	Confectioners' sugar

For the cake, preheat the oven to 375 degrees. Grease a 10x15-inch cake pan. Line with waxed paper and grease the waxed paper. Beat the eggs with a wooden spoon in a large bowl until pale yellow. Add the sugar, pumpkin, baking soda, salt, cinnamon and flour and mix well. Pour the batter evenly into the prepared pan. Bake for 15 minutes.

Dust a clean kitchen towel with sifted confectioners' sugar. Invert the warm cake onto the towel. Remove the waxed paper. Roll the warm cake in the towel as for a jellyroll from the short side and place on a wire rack to cool.

For the filling, combine 2 cups confectioners' sugar, butter, cream cheese and vanilla in a mixing bowl and beat until light and fluffy.

To assemble, unroll the cooled cake carefully and remove the towel. Spread the filling to the edge and roll the cake. Cut into 1-inch slices, sprinkle with additional confectioners' sugar and serve. The cake will keep, covered in the refrigerator, for 2 days.

Dulce de Leche Cheesecake

Dulce de leche is a caramel-like delight with origins in South America. This slightly sweet cheesecake with chocolate glaze offers an elegant taste for a dessert buffet.

YIELD: 64 PIECES

Dulce de Leche

1	cup heavy cream
1	cup packed dark brown sugar
1/2	cup sweetened condensed milk
1/2	teaspoon vanilla extract

Crust

1	cup finely crushed wheat crackers or graham crackers
2	tablespoons sugar
3	tablespoons butter, melted

Filling

1	teaspoon unflavored gelatin
1/4	cup milk
8	ounces cream cheese, softened
2	eggs
3/8	teaspoon salt

Chocolate Glaze

3	ounces bittersweet chocolate, coarsely chopped
1/4	cup (1/2 stick) unsalted butter, chopped
2	teaspoons light corn syrup

For the dulce de leche, combine the heavy cream and brown sugar in a heavy saucepan over medium heat. Cook for 2 to 3 minutes or until the sugar dissolves, stirring constantly. Bring to a boil and boil for 5 to 10 minutes or until the mixture is reduced to 1 cup, stirring occasionally. Stir in the condensed milk and vanilla. Remove from the heat and let stand until cool.

For the crust, preheat the oven to 325 degrees. Line the bottom and sides of an 8-inch glass baking pan by crisscrossing 2 sheets of foil, leaving a slight overhang to create handles.

Combine the cracker crumbs and sugar in a small bowl. Add the butter and mix well. Press the mixture evenly over the bottom of the prepared pan. Bake for 10 minutes. Remove the pan to a wire rack to cool completely.

For the filling, sprinkle the gelatin over the milk in a small bowl and let stand for 2 minutes or until the gelatin is soft. Combine with the cream cheese, eggs and salt in a mixing bowl and beat well at medium speed. Stir in 1 cup dulce de leche, reserving the remaining dulce de leche for another use.

Pour the filling over the cooled crust, smoothing with a spatula. Place the pan in a larger baking pan. Add hot water to reach halfway up the outside of the smaller pan. Bake for 45 minutes or just until set. Remove to a wire rack to cool completely. Chill, covered, for 6 hours to 3 days.

For the glaze, combine the chocolate, butter and corn syrup in a small microwaveable bowl. Microwave, covered loosely with plastic wrap, on High for 30 seconds. Stir the mixture and microwave for 30 seconds longer. Whisk until smooth. Pour over the cheesecake, swirling the pan to coat evenly. Chill, uncovered, for 30 minutes. Do not prepare the glaze more than 2 hours prior to serving.

Lift the cheesecake from the pan using the foil handles. Cut the cake into 1-inch squares, wiping the knife after each cut for the best presentation. Arrange on a platter and serve.

New York Cheesecake with Strawberry Glaze

YIELD: 16 SERVINGS

Cheesecake

2½	cups shortbread cookie crumbs
6	tablespoons butter, melted
40	ounces cream cheese, softened
1¾	cups sugar
3	tablespoons flour
¼	teaspoon salt
1½	teaspoons vanilla extract
4	eggs
2	egg yolks
¼	cup heavy cream
1	cup sour cream
2	tablespoons confectioners' sugar

Strawberry Glaze

12	ounces seedless raspberry preserves
1	tablespoon cornstarch
¼	cup Triple Sec
¼	cup water
1	quart fresh strawberries, hulled and sliced

For the cheesecake, preheat the oven to 350 degrees. Grease the side of a 10-inch springform pan. Combine the cookie crumbs and butter in a bowl and mix well. Press over the bottom of the prepared pan. Bake for 10 minutes.

Increase the oven temperature to 450 degrees. Beat the cream cheese in a large mixing bowl until smooth. Add the sugar, flour, salt and vanilla and beat until smooth. Add the eggs and egg yolks 1 at a time, beating well after each addition. Stir in the heavy cream. Spoon over the prepared crust. Bake for 12 minutes. Reduce the temperature to 300 degrees and bake for 55 minutes. Cool on a wire rack for 1 hour. Remove the side of the pan and let cool completely. Combine the sour cream and confectioners' sugar in a small bowl and whisk until smooth. Spoon onto the cooled cheesecake, leaving a ½-inch border.

For the glaze, combine a small amount of the preserves with the cornstarch in a medium saucepan and mix well. Stir in the remaining preserves, Triple Sec and water. Cook over medium heat for 5 to 10 minutes or until the glaze is thick and clear, stirring occasionally. Remove from the heat and let cool to lukewarm, stirring occasionally. Stir in the strawberries. Slice the cheesecake and spoon the glaze over each slice.

Cherry Vanilla Lattice Pie

YIELD: 8 SERVINGS

Flaky Pie Crust

2½	cups flour
1½	tablespoons sugar
1¼	teaspoons salt
⅔	cup shortening, frozen and cut into ½-inch pieces
½	cup (1 stick) cold unsalted butter, cut into ½-inch pieces
6	tablespoons ice water
2	teaspoons apple cider vinegar

Pie

1	cup plus 2 tablespoons sugar
¼	cup quick-cooking tapioca
½	teaspoon salt
¼	teaspoon cinnamon
½	teaspoon grated orange zest
6	to 7 cups fresh or frozen tart cherries, pitted
2	to 3 teaspoons vanilla extract
	Ice cream

For the crust, combine the flour, sugar and salt in a food processor. Add the shortening and butter and pulse until the mixture resembles coarse meal. Spoon into a bowl. Combine the water and vinegar in a bowl and mix well. Pour over the flour mixture. Mix with a fork until the mixture forms a ball, adding additional water, 1 teaspoon at a time, if necessary. Shape the dough into 2 balls. Flatten each into a disk. Chill, wrapped in plastic wrap, for 30 minutes to 3 days.

Roll 1 dough disk into an 11-inch circle on a lightly floured surface. Fit into a 9-inch pie plate, leaving a ¾-inch overhang. Roll out the remaining dough into an 11-inch circle on a lightly floured surface. Cut into 1-inch-wide strips. Place a piece of waxed paper on a baking sheet. Weave the strips in a lattice pattern on the waxed paper. Chill in the refrigerator or freezer for 20 minutes or until firm.

For the pie, cover the lower oven rack with foil. Preheat the oven to 400 degrees. Combine the sugar, tapioca, salt, cinnamon and orange zest in a small bowl and mix well. Cook the cherries in a large heavy skillet over medium-high heat for 2 to 5 minutes or until the cherries are slightly soft and the juices begin to run. Remove with a slotted spoon to a bowl. Add the tapioca mixture to the juice in the skillet and bring to a simmer. Simmer for 3 minutes or until thickened, stirring constantly. The tapioca will remain uncooked. Add to the cherries and mix well. Stir in the vanilla. Let stand until cool. Pour into the pastry-lined pie plate. Moisten the edge of the pastry with cold water. Top with the lattice. Let stand for 10 minutes. Trim the edge and crimp together. Brush with cold water and sprinkle lightly with sugar. Bake on the middle oven rack for 40 to 45 minutes or until the edge is golden brown and the filling begins to bubble. Cool on a wire rack. Serve warm or at room temperature with ice cream.

Just a bowl of cherries.

No place on earth produces as many tart red cherries as Michigan. We know they're not just good, they're good for you— rich in antioxidants and pain-relieving compounds. Fun fact: There are about 7,000 tart cherries on an average tree, enough for 28 pies!

Just peachy.

Michigan ranks

fourth in the nation

in peach production,

and our Red Haven

peaches have

become the most

widely planted variety

in the world. Tip:

Select peaches that

are free from bruises

and decay and not

too soft or overripe.

Be sure they have

that wonderful

"peach" smell.

Grandma's Dutch Apple Pie

YIELD: 8 SERVINGS

Crumble Topping

1½	cups flour
1	cup sugar
⅔	cup cold butter, cut into ½-inch pieces

Apple Pie

8	cups sliced peeled Jonathan apples
¾	cup sugar
1½	teaspoons cinnamon
1	tablespoon flour
1	unbaked (9-inch) pie shell
	Ice cream or whipped cream

For the topping, combine the flour and sugar in a bowl. Cut in the butter with a pastry blender or 2 forks until the mixture is the size of small peas.

For the pie, preheat the oven to 425 degrees. Combine the apples, sugar, cinnamon and flour in a large bowl. Spoon into the pie shell. Sprinkle with the topping. Bake for 15 minutes. Reduce the heat to 350 degrees. Bake for 45 to 50 minutes or until the apples are tender and the topping is light brown. Serve warm with ice cream or whipped cream.

Peaches and Cream Pie

(PICTURED ON PAGE 150)

This effortless pie becomes an incredibly rich and creamy delicacy right before your eyes.

YIELD: 8 SERVINGS

4	cups sliced peeled fresh peaches
1	unbaked (9-inch) pie shell
	Pinch of salt
1	teaspoon lemon juice
⅓	cup butter, softened
⅓	cup flour
1	cup sugar
1	egg, slightly beaten
¼	teaspoon vanilla extract

Preheat the oven to 425 degrees. Place the peaches in the pie shell. Sprinkle with the salt and lemon juice. Cream the butter, flour and sugar in a mixing bowl. Add the egg and vanilla and mix well. Spread over the peaches.

Bake for 12 minutes. Reduce the heat to 350 degrees. Bake for 40 to 45 minutes or until golden brown and bubbling. Let stand until cool. You may reduce the amount of sugar to taste if the peaches are very sweet.

Deep-Dish Strawberry Cream Pie

(PICTURED ON PAGE 150)

It's awfully difficult to improve upon a summertime classic, but this nutty crust flavor paired with the succulent, sweet strawberries will leave you pleasantly surprised.

YIELD: 8 TO 10 SERVINGS

Pretzel Crust

1½	cups crushed pretzels
½	cup (1 stick) butter, melted
¼	cup sugar

Strawberry Pie

3	ounces cream cheese, softened
3	tablespoons confectioners' sugar
2	teaspoons orange liqueur
7	to 8 cups strawberries, hulled
1	cup sugar
3	tablespoons cornstarch
¾	cup water
½	teaspoon vanilla extract
1	cup whipping cream

For the crust, preheat the oven to 350 degrees. Combine the pretzels, butter and sugar in a bowl and mix well. Press over the bottom and halfway up the side of a 9-inch deep-dish pie plate. Bake for 10 minutes or until light brown. Let stand until cool.

For the pie, beat the cream cheese and confectioners' sugar in a mixing bowl until smooth. Add the liqueur and mix well. Spread evenly over the bottom and partially up the side of the cooled crust. Arrange 5 to 6 cups of the strawberries, stem side down, on the cream cheese layer.

Mash the remaining strawberries. Combine with the sugar in a saucepan over medium heat. Bring to a boil, stirring frequently. Whisk together the cornstarch, water and vanilla in a small bowl. Add to the strawberry mixture gradually, stirring constantly. Reduce the heat and simmer for 8 to 10 minutes or until thickened, stirring constantly. Remove from the heat and strain, discarding the pulp. Pour evenly over the strawberry layer. Chill, uncovered, for 4 to 6 hours.

Beat the whipping cream in a mixing bowl until soft peaks form. Spread over the pie, leaving a 1- to 2-inch edge. Garnish with 2 sliced strawberries and mint leaves.

Tiramisu Toffee Trifle Pie

(PICTURED ON PAGE 150)

YIELD: 8 TO 10 SERVINGS

1½	tablespoons instant espresso granules
¾	cup warm water
½	Cream Cheese Pound Cake (below)
8	ounces mascarpone cheese, softened
½	cup confectioners' sugar
½	cup chocolate syrup
12	ounces frozen whipped topping, thawed
2	English toffee candy bars, coarsely chopped

Dissolve the espresso granules in the water in a small bowl. Let stand until cool. Cut the pound cake into 14 slices and cut the slices into halves crosswise. Arrange in the bottom and up the side of a 9-inch deep-dish pie plate. Drizzle the espresso mixture over the cake.

Beat the mascarpone cheese, sugar and chocolate syrup in a mixing bowl until smooth. Add 2½ cups of the whipped topping and beat until light and fluffy.

Spread over the cake layer. Chill, loosely covered with plastic wrap, for 8 hours.

Dollop the remaining whipped topping in a decorative pattern around the edge of the pie. Sprinkle with the candy bar pieces, slice and serve.

Cream Cheese Pound Cake

YIELD: 10 TO 12 SERVINGS

1½	cups (3 sticks) butter, softened
8	ounces cream cheese, softened
3	cups sugar
6	eggs
3	cups flour
⅛	teaspoon salt
1	tablespoon vanilla extract

Preheat the oven to 300 degrees. Beat the butter and cream cheese in a mixing bowl until smooth. Add the sugar gradually, beating to mix well. Add the eggs, 1 at a time, beating well after each addition.

Combine the flour and salt in a bowl. Add to the creamed mixture gradually, beating at low speed constantly. Stir in the vanilla. Pour into a greased and floured 8-inch springform pan. Bake for 1 hour and 40 minutes or until a wooden pick inserted in the center comes out clean. Cool in the pan on a wire rack for 10 to 15 minutes. Remove from the pan and cool completely on a wire rack. May be stored, wrapped in plastic wrap, for 1 week.

Raspberry-Topped Chocolate Tart with Pecan Crust

YIELD: 6 TO 8 SERVINGS

2	cups pecans, toasted
6	tablespoons brown sugar
1/4	teaspoon cinnamon
1/4	cups (1/2 stick) butter, melted
3/4	cup heavy cream
6	ounces bittersweet chocolate, chopped
1	pint raspberries
1/4	cup seedless raspberry jam
	Whipped cream

Preheat the oven to 325 degrees. Process the pecans, brown sugar and cinnamon in a food processor until finely ground. Add the butter and process just until moistened. Press over the bottom and up the side of a 9-inch tart pan with a removable bottom. Bake for 30 minutes or until golden brown and firm. Cool on a wire rack.

Bring the heavy cream to a simmer in a heavy saucepan over medium heat. Remove from the heat. Add the chocolate and stir until melted and smooth.

Pour evenly over the cooled crust. Chill, uncovered, for 1 hour or until set. Chill, covered, for up to 1 day if not serving immediately.

Arrange the raspberries, stem side down, on the chocolate layer. Melt the jam in a heavy saucepan over low heat, stirring constantly. Brush over the raspberries. Slice and serve with a dollop of whipped cream.

Spotlight: Interlochen Center for the Arts

This 1,200-acre campus in Northern Michigan is one of America's true cultural treasures— and the country's premier site for young musicians, dancers, actors, visual artists, and writers to explore and develop their talents. Alumni include actor Linda Hunt, dancer Peter Sparling, singer Jessye Norman, and broadcaster Mike Wallace.

Strawberry Lemon Tart with Shortbread Crust

YIELD: 10 SERVINGS

Lemon Custard

2	eggs
1/2	cup sugar
3	tablespoons fresh lemon juice
1/4	cup (1/2 stick) unsalted butter
1 1/2	teaspoons grated lemon zest

Shortbread Crust

1 1/2	cups flour
3	tablespoons sugar
1/4	teaspoon salt
1/2	cup (1 stick) chilled butter, cut into 1/2-inch pieces
2	tablespoons heavy cream
1	egg yolk

Assembly

1 1/2	quarts fresh strawberries, hulled
1/2	cup seedless strawberry preserves
	Sweetened whipped cream

For the custard, whisk together the eggs, sugar and lemon juice in a small heavy saucepan over medium heat. Add the butter and lemon zest and cook for 8 to 10 minutes or until the mixture thickens to a pudding consistency, stirring constantly. Remove to a small bowl. Chill, covered, for 2 hours or longer.

For the crust, combine the flour, sugar and salt in a large bowl. Cut in the butter until the mixture resembles coarse meal. Add the heavy cream and egg yolk and mix with a wooden spoon just until moistened, adding additional cream if the mixture is too dry. Roll into a ball. Flatten into a disk. Chill, wrapped in plastic wrap, for 1 hour. Roll into a 13-inch circle on a lightly floured surface. Fit into a 9-inch tart pan with a removable bottom and trim the excess dough to 1/2 inch.

Fold inward and press to form a double edge. Pierce the dough several times with a fork. Chill for 1 hour. Preheat the oven to 400 degrees. Bake for 20 minutes or until golden brown. Cool completely on a wire rack.

For the assembly, spread the custard over the crust. Arrange the strawberries, stem side down, over the custard. Heat the preserves in a small saucepan until warm and thin. Brush over the strawberries. Chill, uncovered, for 1 to 6 hours or until the glaze sets. Release the tart from the pan. Slice and serve with a dollop of whipped cream.

Martha's Vineyard Wine Selection:
Joseph Phelps Eisrebe

Layered Berry Torte

This special-occasion cake can be made early in the day and assembled just prior to serving.

YIELD: 10 SERVINGS

Cake

½	cup (1 stick) butter, softened
¾	cup sugar
4	egg yolks, beaten
1	teaspoon vanilla extract
1	cup cake flour
1	teaspoon baking powder
5	tablespoons milk

Meringue

4	egg whites
1	teaspoon cream of tartar
1	cup sugar

Assembly

1	pint whipping cream
2	tablespoons sugar
1	quart raspberries
1	quart strawberries, hulled and sliced

For the cake, preheat the oven to 325 degrees. Grease two 9-inch cake pans. Line the bottoms of the pans with waxed paper. Grease the waxed paper. Cream the butter and sugar in a large mixing bowl until light and fluffy. Add the egg yolks and vanilla and mix well. Combine the flour and baking powder in a small bowl. Add to the creamed mixture alternately with the milk, beating well after each addition. Pour into the prepared cake pans.

For the meringue, beat the egg whites and cream of tartar in a mixing bowl until stiff peaks form. Add the sugar gradually, beating until the sugar is dissolved. Spread half the meringue over the cake batter in 1 pan. Spread the remaining half of the meringue over the cake batter in the remaining pan. Bake for 35 minutes or until the meringue is light brown. Cool in the pans on a wire rack. Remove from the pans and let stand, loosely covered with plastic wrap, until ready to assemble.

For the assembly, whip the cream in a mixing bowl. Add the sugar gradually, beating constantly until stiff peaks form. Place 1 cake layer, meringue side up, on a cake platter. Spread half the whipped cream over the top. Spoon half the raspberries and half the strawberries over the whipped cream. Top with the remaining cake layer, meringue side up. Spread with the remaining whipped cream and top with the remaining raspberries and strawberries. Slice and serve immediately.

Chocolate Chameleon Torte

This recipe, which must be started one day prior to serving, was developed by Mike Schoenbom, Executive Chef, and Ginnie Burger, Pastry Chef, Egypt Valley Country Club, and can be prepared in a variety of delightful variations, as noted on these two pages.

YIELD: 10 TO 12 SERVINGS

16	ounces semisweet chocolate
1/2	cup (1 stick) plus 2 tablespoons butter
5	eggs
1	tablespoon sugar
1 1/4	tablespoons sifted flour
2	ounces your favorite flavoring or liqueur
	Desired topping and garnish

Preheat the oven to 425 degrees. Melt the chocolate and butter in a double boiler over simmering water, stirring until smooth. Pour into a large bowl and let stand until slightly cool.

Whisk the eggs and sugar in a double boiler over simmering water until the mixture is warm and pale yellow. Pour into a large bowl and beat at high speed for 5 to 10 minutes or until the volume is tripled. Fold the egg mixture, flour and flavoring into the chocolate mixture.

Pour into a greased and floured 9-inch springform pan. Bake for 18 to 20 minutes or until a wooden pick inserted in the center comes out clean. Cool in the pan for 8 hours.

Martha's Vineyard Wine Selection:
Rosemount "Old Benson" Tawny Port

Chocolate Chambord Torte

YIELD: 10 TO 12 SERVINGS

1	Chocolate Chameleon Torte recipe (above)
4	ounces Chambord or other raspberry liqueur
2	cups fresh raspberries
1	cup confectioners' sugar
3	tablespoons fresh lemon juice
1/2	cup fresh raspberries

Prepare and bake the Chocolate Chameleon Torte as directed using 2 ounces Chambord. Cool in the pan for 8 hours.

Purée 2 ounces Chambord, 2 cups raspberries, the confectioners' sugar and lemon juice in a blender. Strain the sauce and discard the seeds. Chill, covered, until ready to serve.

To serve, place the torte on a serving plate and remove the side of the pan. Cut into wedges. Drizzle each piece with the raspberry sauce and top with 1/2 cup raspberries.

Chocolate Torte with Caramelized Bananas

YIELD: 10 TO 12 SERVINGS

1	Chocolate Chameleon Torte recipe (page 166)
2	ounces Grand Marnier or Cointreau
12	ounces white chocolate, chopped
¾	cup heavy cream, chilled
1	teaspoon vanilla extract
1	teaspoon grated orange peel
¾	cup whipping cream, chilled
3	pasteurized egg whites
4	ripe bananas
¼	cup sugar
2	teaspoons fresh lemon juice
1	cup bittersweet chocolate sauce
2	tablespoons chopped macadamia nuts

Prepare and bake the Chocolate Chameleon Torte as directed using 2 ounces Grand Marnier. Cool in the pan for 8 hours.

Combine the white chocolate and heavy cream in a large microwaveable bowl and microwave on High until the mixture is melted and smooth, stirring every 30 seconds. Stir in the vanilla and orange peel. Let stand until cooled to room temperature.

Beat the whipping cream in a mixing bowl until stiff peaks form. Beat the egg whites in a mixing bowl until stiff peaks form. Fold the egg whites into the white chocolate mixture. Fold in the whipped cream. Spoon over the torte. Chill, covered, for 8 hours.

Preheat the broiler. Line a baking sheet with foil and spray the foil with cooking spray. Slice the bananas into ½-inch pieces. Combine with the sugar and lemon juice in a bowl and toss to coat. Arrange in a single layer on the prepared baking sheet. Broil for 3 to 4 minutes or until the bananas begin to caramelize. Remove from the oven and let stand until cool.

Place the torte on a serving plate and remove the side of the pan. Top with the bananas. Drizzle with the chocolate sauce and sprinkle with the macadamia nuts. Slice and serve.

Mocha Torte with Crème Anglaise

YIELD: 10 TO 12 SERVINGS

2	teaspoons instant coffee granules
1	ounce (⅛ cup) water
1	Chocolate Chameleon Torte recipe (page 166)
1	ounce rum
4	egg yolks
⅓	cup sugar
1	teaspoon vanilla extract
1	cup heavy cream
1	cup milk
½	ounce bittersweet chocolate, shaved

Dissolve the coffee granules in the water in a small bowl. Prepare and bake the Chocolate Chameleon Torte as directed using the coffee and 1 ounce rum. Cool in the pan for 8 hours.

Combine the egg yolks with the sugar in a double boiler over very hot, but not boiling, water and whisk until blended. Add the vanilla, heavy cream and milk gradually, stirring constantly. Cook for 10 to 12 minutes or until thickened, stirring constantly. Chill, covered, until ready to serve.

Place the torte on a serving plate and remove the side of the pan. Cut into wedges. Spoon 2 tablespoons of the crème onto each dessert plate. Top each with 1 slice of the torte and some of the chocolate shavings and serve.

Bananas Foster en Croûte

YIELD: 2 SERVINGS

½	sheet frozen puff pastry
2	green-tip bananas
5	tablespoons butter
¼	cup packed brown sugar
1	teaspoon cinnamon
1	tablespoon banana liqueur
2	ounces dark rum
¼	cup chopped pecans
2	scoops vanilla bean ice cream
	Cinnamon

Preheat the oven to 400 degrees. Cut the pastry sheet into two 5-inch squares and place on a parchment-lined baking sheet. Bake for 12 to 15 minutes or until the pastry is puffed and golden brown.

Slice the bananas into halves lengthwise. Melt the butter in a sauté pan over medium-high heat. Reduce the heat to low and add the brown sugar, 1 teaspoon cinnamon and banana liqueur and mix well. Cook until the mixture is of a thin caramel consistency, stirring constantly. Add the bananas and spoon the mixture over the bananas to coat. Add the rum and pecans and cook for 3 to 4 minutes or until the alcohol has evaporated, turning the bananas once. Remove from the heat.

Cut a 2-inch square in the center of each pastry sheet. Remove the small squares and reserve for garnish. Place each large pastry square onto a serving plate. Spoon a scoop of ice cream onto the center of each pastry. Arrange 2 banana slices over each scoop of ice cream. Spoon the pecan mixture over the top. Sprinkle lightly with cinnamon. Garnish with mint sprigs and the reserved pastry squares.

Who's that blonde? Visitors often remark on the number of blue-eyed, blonde-haired residents in West Michigan. It's in our genes— Dutch is the largest nationality group in Grand Rapids, and the lakeshore city of Holland has the largest Dutch population outside of Europe. Credit a wave of immigration dating back to the 19th century.

Crème Brûlée

This recipe was provided by Brett Hurley, Executive Chef, Aquinas College.

YIELD: 8 SERVINGS

2½ cups heavy cream

5 egg yolks

3 eggs

¾ cup packed brown sugar

½ teaspoon salt

2 teaspoons vanilla extract

½ cup packed brown sugar

Bring the heavy cream almost to a boil in a saucepan over medium heat. Combine the egg yolks, eggs and ¾ cup brown sugar in a large bowl and mix well. Add the cream slowly, whisking constantly. Do not add the cream too quickly as it will cause the mixture to curdle. Add the salt and vanilla and mix well.

Preheat the oven to 320 degrees. Arrange 8 ramekins in a large baking dish. Pour the cream mixture into the ramekins. Add enough hot water to reach halfway up the sides of the ramekins. Cover the ramekins loosely with foil. Bake for 25 to 40 minutes or just until set, removing the foil 5 minutes prior to the end of the baking time. Cool on a wire rack for 20 minutes. Chill, covered, until 20 minutes prior to serving.

To serve, sprinkle the brûlée evenly with ½ cup brown sugar. Broil or use a propane torch for 1 to 2 minutes or until the sugar melts and begins to form a crystallized crust. Serve warm or at room temperature.

You may add ½ pint fresh raspberries and 4 ounces chopped white chocolate, ½ pint sliced strawberries, 2 peeled and sliced fresh peaches, 5 ounces crushed pineapple or 4 ounces chopped semisweet chocolate to the cream mixture before filling the ramekins if desired.

Ice Cream Sundae Cake

YIELD: 12 SERVINGS

1½	cups flour
1½	cups finely chopped pecans
½	cup quick-cooking oats
½	cup packed brown sugar
¾	cup (1½ sticks) butter, softened
1	(12-ounce) jar caramel topping
1	(16-ounce) jar fudge topping
1	gallon vanilla ice cream, softened
½	gallon chocolate ice cream, softened

Preheat the oven to 400 degrees. Combine the flour, pecans, oats, brown sugar and butter in a bowl and mix well. Press over the bottom of a 9x13-inch baking pan. Bake for 15 minutes. Let stand until cool. Crumble the mixture into a bowl. Press ⅔ of the crumbled mixture over the bottom of the baking pan, reserving the remaining ⅓ of the mixture.

Warm the caramel topping in a small saucepan over medium-low heat. Warm the fudge topping in a small saucepan over medium-low heat. Drizzle ⅔ of the caramel topping over the prepared layer.

Drizzle with ¾ of the fudge topping. Spread the vanilla ice cream over the prepared layers. Top with tablespoonfuls of the chocolate ice cream, pushing the chocolate ice cream into the vanilla ice cream to create chocolate pockets. Smooth the top. Sprinkle with the reserved crumbled mixture. Drizzle with the remaining caramel topping and remaining fudge topping. Freeze, covered, for several hours. To serve, let stand at room temperature to soften. Cut into squares. You may store in the freezer for up to 1 week.

Easy Ice Cream

This excuse for play is courtesy of the Grand Rapids Children's Museum.

YIELD: 1 SERVING

½	cup milk
1	tablespoon sugar
¼	teaspoon vanilla extract
½	cup rock salt

Combine the milk, sugar and vanilla in a pint-size resealable plastic bag. Place the rock salt in a gallon-size resealable plastic bag. Add ice to fill ¼ of the bag. Seal the smaller bag and place in the larger bag.

Seal the larger bag and shake for 5 minutes or longer over a trash can to catch any spills. Remove the small bag and enjoy the ice cream.

Kahlúa Mocha Mousse

YIELD: 4 SERVINGS

Mousse

3	ounces bittersweet chocolate
1½	ounces unsweetened chocolate
2	tablespoons Kahlúa
2	tablespoons very strong brewed coffee
2	egg yolks
3	tablespoons confectioners' sugar
2	pasteurized egg whites
1	pinch of salt
1	pinch of cream of tartar
1	tablespoon confectioners' sugar
¾	cup whipping cream

Whipped Cream Garnish

¼	cup whipping cream
1	tablespoon confectioners' sugar
1	tablespoon Kahlúa

For the mousse, combine the bittersweet chocolate, unsweetened chocolate and Kahlúa in a small glass bowl. Microwave for 2 to 3 minutes or until melted, stirring occasionally. Let stand to cool for 10 minutes.

Combine the coffee, egg yolks and confectioners' sugar in the top of a double boiler over simmering water. Cook for 6 minutes or to 160 degrees on a candy thermometer, whisking constantly until the mixture is frothy. Pour into a large mixing bowl and beat for 3 minutes or until the mixture is thick and cool. Fold in the chocolate mixture.

Combine the egg whites and salt in a mixing bowl and beat until frothy. Add the cream of tartar and beat until soft peaks form. Add the confectioners' sugar gradually, beating until stiff peaks form.

Stir ¼ of the egg white mixture into the chocolate mixture using a wooden spoon. Fold in the remaining egg white mixture.

Beat the whipping cream in a mixing bowl until stiff peaks form. Fold gently into the chocolate mixture. Pour into 4 ramekins. Chill, covered, for 2 to 8 hours.

For the garnish, beat the whipping cream in a chilled metal bowl until soft peaks form. Add the confectioners' sugar and Kahlúa and beat until stiff peaks form. Serve the mousse with a dollop of the whipped cream and garnish with unsweetened chocolate shavings.

Berries and Mint with a Splash

(PICTURED ON PAGE 150)

YIELD: 4 SERVINGS

1	pint strawberries, hulled and halved
1	pint blueberries, stemmed
2	teaspoons orange or raspberry liqueur (optional)
½	cup loosely packed chopped fresh mint leaves
4	scoops vanilla ice cream

Combine the strawberries and blueberries in a large bowl. Sprinkle with the liqueur and mint and toss gently to combine. Chill, covered, for 1 to 2 hours.

To serve, place the scoops of ice cream in small bowls. Spoon the fruit mixture over the top.

Martha's Vineyard
Wine Selection:
R.L. Buller Fine Muscat

Million-dollar mint. Michigan is a large producer of mint and distiller of mint oil, used in everything from toothpaste to chewing gum to medicine. Fun fact: One pound of mint yields almost 150,000 sticks of chewing gum!

Lemon Cloud Dessert

YIELD: 9 SERVINGS

1	(12-ounce) package vanilla wafers, crushed
3	pasteurized egg yolks
⅔	cup sugar
	Juice of 1 lemon
	Grated zest of 1 lemon
8	ounces whipping cream
3	pasteurized egg whites

Sprinkle ⅔ of the cookie crumbs evenly over the bottom of an 8x8-inch glass dish. Beat the egg yolks in a medium bowl until lemon-colored. Add the sugar and mix well. Stir in the lemon juice and lemon zest.

Beat the whipping cream in a small bowl until stiff peaks form. Fold the whipped cream into the lemon mixture. Beat the egg whites in a small bowl until stiff peaks form. Fold into the lemon mixture. Spread evenly over the prepared layer. Sprinkle with the remaining cookie crumbs. Freeze, covered, up to 8 hours. Let stand at room temperature for 10 minutes before serving.

Pecan Shortbread Squares

YIELD: 24 SQUARES

Crust

1	cup plus 2 tablespoons (2¼ sticks) unsalted butter, softened
¾	cups packed brown sugar
3	cups flour, sifted
½	teaspoon salt

Pecan Filling

½	cup packed brown sugar
½	cup (1 stick) unsalted butter
3	tablespoons honey
2	tablespoons light corn syrup
2	tablespoons heavy cream
2	tablespoons sugar
½	teaspoon vanilla extract
2½	cups pecan halves
½	teaspoon salt

For the crust, cream the butter and brown sugar in a bowl until light and fluffy. Combine the flour and salt in a bowl. Add the flour mixture to the creamed mixture 1 cup at a time, mixing well after each addition. The dough will be crumbly. Press the dough evenly over the bottom and ¾ inch up the sides of a 9x13-inch baking pan. Poke holes evenly all over the dough with a fork. Chill, covered, for 20 minutes. Preheat the oven to 375 degrees. Bake for 18 to 20 minutes or until the crust is golden brown. Remove from the oven and let cool slightly.

For the filling, reduce the oven temperature to 325 degrees. Combine the brown sugar, butter, honey, corn syrup, heavy cream and sugar in a heavy saucepan over medium-high heat. Bring to a boil and boil for 1 minute or until the mixture coats the back of a wooden spoon, stirring constantly. Stir in the vanilla. Remove from the heat. Add the pecans and salt and stir just until the pecans are coated. Pour evenly over the crust. Bake for 15 to 20 minutes or until bubbly. Remove the pan to a wire rack to cool completely. Cut into squares and serve at room temperature.

Triple-Chocolate Brownies

YIELD: 24 BROWNIES

Melting chocolate?
Do it sloooowly. If
you're using a double
boiler, water should
not touch the bottom
of the upper pan.
Bring the water to
a simmer, turn off
the heat and add the
chocolate. If using
a microwave, place
chocolate in a glass
bowl, zap it on High
for 30 seconds and
stir. Repeat as needed.

5	ounces semisweet or bittersweet chocolate, chopped
2	ounces unsweetened chocolate, chopped
1/2	cup (1 stick) unsalted butter, softened
3	tablespoons Dutch-processed cocoa powder
3	eggs
1 1/4	cups sugar
2	teaspoons vanilla extract
1/2	teaspoon salt
1	cup flour

Adjust the oven rack to the lower-middle position and preheat the oven to 350 degrees. Spray an 8-inch baking pan with nonstick cooking spray. Line the bottom and sides of the pan by crisscrossing 2 pieces of foil, leaving a slight overhang to create handles. Spray the foil with nonstick cooking spray.

Melt the semisweet chocolate, unsweetened chocolate and butter in a bowl set over a pan of hot, but not boiling, water, stirring occasionally until blended. Whisk in the cocoa powder. Remove from the heat and let cool slightly.

Combine the eggs, sugar, vanilla and salt in a bowl and whisk until blended. Whisk in the warm chocolate mixture. Stir in the flour with a wooden spoon just until combined. Pour evenly into the prepared pan. Bake for 35 to 40 minutes or until slightly puffed and a wooden pick inserted in the center comes out with a small amount of very moist crumbs. Cool on a wire rack. Lift from the pan using the foil handles and cut into squares. Chill, wrapped in plastic wrap, for up to 5 days.

Butter Cookies with Lemon Icing

The flavor of these delicate cookies improves with age.

YIELD: 4 DOZEN COOKIES

Butter Cookies

1	cup (2 sticks) butter, softened
1/3	cup confectioners' sugar
2	cups flour
2/3	cup chopped pecans

Lemon Icing

1	cup confectioners' sugar
2	tablespoons butter
1	tablespoon lemon juice

For the cookies, cream the butter and confectioners' sugar in a bowl until light and fluffy. Stir in the flour. Chill, covered, for 1 hour. Preheat the oven to 350 degrees. Arrange the pecans in a single layer on a sheet of waxed paper. Shape the dough into 1-inch balls. Place on the pecans. Flatten with a floured cookie press. Arrange, pecan side down, on an ungreased cookie sheet. Bake for 12 to 14 minutes or until golden brown. Remove the cookies to a wire rack to cool.

For the icing, combine the confectioners' sugar, butter and lemon juice in a bowl and mix well. Spread the icing over the tops of the cooled cookies. The cookies will keep, stored in an airtight container, for up to 1 week.

Chocolate Toffee Cookies

(PICTURED ON PAGE 152)

Leave some of the toffee pieces in large chunks to add extra interest to these cookies.

YIELD: 18 COOKIES

16	ounces bittersweet or semisweet chocolate, chopped
¼	cup (½ stick) butter
1¾	cups packed brown sugar
4	eggs
1	tablespoon vanilla extract
½	cup flour
1	teaspoon baking powder
¼	teaspoon salt
7	(1.5-ounce) chocolate-covered English toffee bars, chopped
1	cup chopped toasted walnuts

Combine the chocolate and butter in the top of a double boiler over simmering water and stir until blended. Remove from the heat and let cool to room temperature.

Combine the brown sugar and eggs in a mixing bowl and beat for 5 minutes. Add the chocolate mixture and vanilla and mix well. Whisk together the flour, baking powder and salt in a small bowl. Stir into the chocolate mixture. Stir in the toffee bars and walnuts. Chill, covered, for 1 hour or until the dough is firm.

Preheat the oven to 350 degrees. Drop the batter by ¼ cupfuls 2½ inches apart onto a parchment-lined cookie sheet. Chill the remaining batter until ready to bake. Bake for 15 minutes or until the tops are dry and cracked but the cookies are soft. Cool on the cookie sheet. The cookies are best if eaten right away, but they will keep, stored in an airtight container, for up to 1 week.

Dutch Coins

Crispy, buttery, and spicy, these wafer-thin cookies are a melt-in-your-mouth treat.

YIELD: 6 DOZEN COOKIES

2	cups (4 sticks) butter
2	cups sugar
4	cups flour
4	teaspoons cinnamon
1/2	teaspoon nutmeg
1/2	teaspoon cloves
1/2	teaspoon baking soda
1/4	teaspoon salt
1/2	cup sour cream
1/2	cup sliced almonds

Cream the butter and sugar in a bowl until light and fluffy. Sift together the flour, cinnamon, nutmeg, cloves, baking soda and salt. Add the dry ingredients alternately with the sour cream to the creamed mixture, mixing well after each addition. Stir in the almonds. Knead the dough on a work surface covered with waxed paper to mix well. Shape into a log. Chill, tightly wrapped in waxed paper, for 8 hours.

Preheat the oven to 400 degrees. Cut the dough into 1/8-inch slices and place on an ungreased cookie sheet. Chill the remaining dough until ready to bake. Bake for 7 to 8 minutes or until light brown. Cool on the cookie sheet for 1 minute. Remove to a wire rack to cool completely. You may store the cookies in an airtight container for up to 1 week. You may store the dough, tightly wrapped, in the freezer. Let thaw completely in the refrigerator before baking.

Easy Sour Cherry Lemonade

2 pounds sour cherries, stemmed

1 cup fresh lemon juice

1 cup sugar

2 to 3 cups sparkling water

Blend the cherries in a blender until the skins have broken down enough to create a brightly colored liquid. (Yes, some pits will be coarsely chopped.) Strain into a 2-quart pitcher and discard the solids. Add the lemon juice and sugar. Stir until the sugar is dissolved. Add the sparkling water. Serve over ice.

Crispy Crunchy Chewy Oatmeal Cookies

YIELD: 3 DOZEN COOKIES

1	cup sugar
1	cup packed brown sugar
1	cup (2 sticks) butter, softened
2	eggs
1	teaspoon vanilla extract
1	cup crisp rice cereal
1	cup quick-cooking oats
1	cup coconut
2	cups flour
1	teaspoon baking powder
1	teaspoon baking soda
1/2	teaspoon salt

Preheat the oven to 350 degrees. Cream the sugar, brown sugar and butter in a bowl until light and fluffy. Add the eggs and vanilla and mix well. Combine the cereal, oats, coconut, flour, baking powder, baking soda and salt in a bowl and mix well. Add to the creamed mixture and mix well. Drop by tablespoonfuls 2 inches apart onto a greased cookie sheet.

Bake for 10 to 12 minutes or until light brown. Cool on the cookie sheet for 2 minutes. Remove to a wire rack to cool completely. The cookies will keep, stored in an airtight container, for up to 1 week.

Chocolate Turtles

YIELD: 4 DOZEN TURTLES

1	(14-ounce) package caramels
2	tablespoons butter
2	tablespoons water
2	cups pecan halves
1	cup coarsely chopped pecans
1	cup (6 ounces) semisweet chocolate chips
16	ounces vanilla candy coating

Combine the caramels, butter and water in a heavy saucepan over low heat and cook until blended, stirring frequently. Remove from the heat and stir in the pecan halves and chopped pecans. Let cool for 5 minutes, stirring occasionally. Drop by tablespoonfuls onto lightly greased waxed paper. Chill for 1 hour or freeze for 20 minutes or until firm.

Combine the chocolate chips and candy coating in a heavy saucepan over low heat, stirring until smooth. Spray a wire rack with nonstick cooking spray and place the rack over a large bowl or saucepan.

Arrange several caramel-pecan patties on the rack. Spoon the chocolate mixture over the patties, letting the excess drip into the bowl. Reheat the chocolate to thin if necessary. Remove the turtles to lightly greased waxed paper. Let stand until the chocolate has hardened. Repeat the procedure with the remaining caramel-pecan patties and chocolate. The turtles will keep, stored in an airtight container, at room temperature or in the refrigerator for up to 2 weeks. If chilled, bring to room temperature before serving.

Oatmeal Carmelitas

1½	cups flour
1½	cups quick-cooking oats
1½	cups packed brown sugar
1	egg
½	teaspoon baking soda
½	teaspoon salt
¾	cup (1½ sticks) unsalted butter, chopped
12	ounces (2 cups) semisweet chocolate chips
1	cup chopped walnuts
1	(14-ounce) package caramels
½	cup heavy cream

Preheat the oven to 350 degrees. Combine the flour, oats, brown sugar, egg, baking soda and salt in a food processor and process until well mixed. Add the butter and pulse several times, just until moistened. Press 2/3 of the mixture into a thin layer over the bottom of a greased and floured 9x13-inch baking pan. Chill the remaining oat mixture. Bake for 8 to 10 minutes or until light brown. Sprinkle with the chocolate chips and walnuts.

Heat the caramels and heavy cream in a heavy saucepan over medium-low heat until the caramels are melted, stirring constantly. Drizzle over the baked layer. Sprinkle with the remaining oat mixture. Bake for 20 minutes or until the edges are golden brown. Loosen the edges from the sides of the pan and let stand until cool. Cut into pieces and chill until firm. Serve chilled or at room temperature. The carmelitas will keep, wrapped in plastic wrap, in the refrigerator for up to 1 week.

Easy Caramel Corn

3	bags salted unbuttered microwave popcorn, popped
1	cup (2 sticks) butter
2	cups packed brown sugar
½	cup light corn syrup
½	teaspoon baking soda

Remove the unpopped kernels from the popped corn and place the popped corn in a large brown paper bag. Combine the butter, brown sugar and corn syrup in a medium saucepan over medium-high heat. Bring to a boil and boil for 5 minutes, stirring constantly. Remove from the heat and stir in the baking soda.

Pour the caramel over the popped corn. Close the bag and shake well. Microwave on High for 2 minutes. Remove the bag and shake well. Spread over waxed paper to cool. The caramel will be very hot, so be careful.

Pleasurable Mornings

Unwinding on Sundays
Frittata with Tomatoes and Basil
Cinnamon Cream Cheese Coffee Cake
Sliced Melon
Turkey Sausage Links
Tomato Juice, Coffee, and Tea

Celebrating Mom
Spinach and Cheese Strata with Sourdough
Festive Brunch Fruit Salad
Blueberry Coffee Cake with Coconut Streusel
Freshly Squeezed Orange Juice
Coffee and Tea

Mid-Day Mingles

Summer Picnic Celebration
Smoked Turkey Wraps
Orzo Salad with Snow Peas and Grape Tomatoes
Lemon Basil Potato Salad
Poppy Lime Melon
Whole Wheat Zucchini Bread
Triple-Chocolate Brownies
Lemonade and Iced Tea

Here Comes the Bride-to-Be
Summer Salad with Basil Sauce
Fruit Salad Camembert
Sun-Dried Tomato Bread
Poppy Seed Bread with Almond Glaze
Strawberry Lemon Tart with Shortbread Crust
Iced Tea and Soft Drinks

Let's Do Lunch!
Roasted Chicken Salad
Savory Fruit Salad
Java Spice Bread
Butter Cookies with Lemon Icing
White Wine and Soft Drinks

Evening Excursions

How 'bout a Barbecue?
Grilled Parmesan Lime Chicken
Reeds Lake Spinach Salad
Glazed Corn on the Cob
Roasted Garlic Herb Bread
Deep-Dish Strawberry Cream Pie
White Wine, Ice Cold Beer, and Soft Drinks

An Intimate Affair
Spicy Creole Shrimp
Pear Salad with Raspberry Cream
Beef Tenderloin with Artichoke Spinach Stuffing
Broccoli with Goat Cheese Sauce
Cheddar Cheese Popovers
Bananas Foster en Croûte
Champagne

On-the-Go Family
Mediterranean Chicken
White Rice
Fresh Fruit Kabobs with Yogurt
Oatmeal Carmelitas
Iced Tea and Milk

Poolside Fun
Teriyaki Marinated Steak with Pineapple Salsa
Mixed Berry Salad
Tuscan Pasta Salad
Barbecued Baked Beans
Ice Cream Sundae Cake
Lemonade, Iced Tea, and Soft Drinks

Cocktails on the Terrace
Beef Wellington Tarts
Layered Oriental Appetizer
Garlic Lime Pork Tenderloin on Sourdough
East Indian Cheese Ball
Artichoke Crostini
Two-Tomato Tapas
Cocktails and Soft Drinks

The Junior League of Grand Rapids would like to thank the following people and companies that have provided generous financial support for *Grand Temptations* and our Grand Rapids community.

UNDERWRITER

Mercantile Bank of West Michigan

MAITRE D'

Lear Corporation

Martha's Vineyard, Kameel Chamelly

Perry & Stuursma Law Firm

CHEF DE CUISINE

Natalie and Scott Bernecker

Gretchen L. Bieneman

Mrs. John W. Blodgett

Tamara and Jeffrey Christians

Kim and James Cornetet

Maren Enghauser

Randy and Denise Essenberg

Julie and Steve Rupp

Peter and Joan Secchia

Marilyn Way

S J Wisinski & Company

SOUS CHEF

Mr. and Mrs. Norbert Alexander

Jerold and Dorotha Baum

Meredith Beachler

Beneath the Wreath Committee

Val Bernecker

Taylor and Blake Beusse

BioPharma Worldwide

Sharlene Blynt

Betsy Borre

Janice A. Brander

Jean Brooks

Linda C. Camilli

Kristin Carey

Gretchen Chamberlain

Aina S. Clay

Barb Cleland, Junior League of Lansing

Mary Ann Coroneos

Dave and Dori Couvreur

Margie Darooge

Jan Durr

Barbara Owen Edgerle

Kelly and Ron Elliott

Jay and Val Enghauser

Marilyn and Carlton Failor

Mayor Judy Frey

Jill Louiselle Gantos

Carol Gehrke

Sandra and Dave Gibbs

Laura Glazer

Judy Goebel

Meg Goebel

Dawn M. Granger

Rick L. Gundy, Foster, Gundy & Associates

Diane Holmes Hall

Elizabeth N. Hamm

Karen Y. and Fred D. Hartley

Todd and Hester Hendricks

Jill Hilty

Margaret L. Jack

Patsy Jackson

Phil and Michelle Johnson

Bill and Susan Jones

David and Ann Jones

Elizabeth Junewick

Junior League Happy Hour

Ellen D. Kent

Victoria Tuthill Kimball

Cheryl A. Kirsch and David Lundberg

Jeanne Kohn

Kay Kress

Margaret and Bernard E. Kuhn

Susan Laffrey

Karen Lawrence

Amy Leonard

Pamela and Jeff Liggett

Jan Lippert

Nat and Marcia Love

Suzie MacKeigan

Peggy Magnesen

Cheryl Malinzak

Patricia Marks

Betsy Barkwell Mathiesen

Kate McCarthy

Gayle C. McCorkle

Mary Beth Mead

Herman and Connie Miller

Allison Armstrong Montague

Barbara Edison Moore

Liz Morris

Mary Goodwillie Nelson

Nicola Construction

Ann Owen

Martha J. Porter

Margaret Pyle

Sherri Remmelts

Sue Robert

Michael and Christina Rosloneic

Kim Rossi

Michael and Betty Roth

Susan H. Schrotenboer

Schuler Books

Diana R. Sieger

SiemensDematic

Nancy Skinner

Helen L. Smith

Mary H. Stickney

Karen H. Stokes

Katie Tiggleman

Sue Tiggleman

Virginia Vanderboegh

Patrick and Christine VanHaren

Holly G. VanLeuven

Edith G. Vasu

Sandy VerBeek

Lisbeth and Michael Votruba

Kris and Brian Ward

Bill and Pat Waring

Luella M. Warnshuis

Kathy White

Rebecca Wierda

Nancy J. Williams

David and Kris Wilson

Susan Doolittle Wittenbach

Becky D. Wrigley

A very special thanks to all those who helped make *Grand Temptations* a success. All of you who submitted recipes, tested recipes, contributed to the photography and text, or simply lent a hand when we needed it most – we couldn't have done it without you!

184

Recipe Contributors and Testers

Colleen Lowry Alward
Kathy Andersen
Mary Nell Baldwin
Samantha Barber
Jenny Barnes
Mara Bauman
Meredith Beachler
Ann Marie Bell
Cathie Benoit
Natalie Bernecker
Cheryl Berrodin
Taylor Beusse
Cathy Birbeck
Edith Blodgett
Sharlene Blynt
Sheila Bowen
Jennifer Bowman
Janice Brander
Jean Brooks
Ginnie Burger, Egypt Valley Country Club
Donna Burns
Lisa Buth
Nicole Canfield
Kristin Carey
Eric Chaitin, Rose's
Judy Childress
Tamara Christians
Sally Coburn
Sharon Coe
Mary Colopy
Melissa Conlon
Kim Cornetet
Darlene Crumbaugh
Jeanne Czarnopys
Mary Davies
Cynthia Derks
Patricia Dillenbeck
Dorothy Doolittle
Amy Dozeman
Lynn and Pete Draigh
Jan Durr
Barb Edgerle
Kelly Elliott
Maggie Ellwood
Courtney Enghauser
Jennifer Enghauser
Marni Enghauser
Val Enghauser
Janis Engle
Beth Engstrom
Tim Fairman, Flat River Grill
Maureen Fischer
Mary Beth Fitzgerald

Mrs. Gerald R. (Betty) Ford
Marsha Fowler
Mayor Judy Frey
Joan Stagg Gallagher
Kelly Gatecliff
Bobbie Gilmore
Laura Glazer
Chris Goodrich
Janet Goyne
Susan Grant
Michelle Gumbko
Katherine Klein Gundy
Carla Hansen
Cindy Hanson
Charlene Harmelink
Amy G. Harris
Nancy Hays
Laurie Hebert
Audrey Schrey-Heckwolf
Martin J. Hillard
Josef Huber, Amway Grand Plaza
Melissa Hungerford
Brett Hurley, Aquinas College
Murry Idema
Wendy Jacobs
Melissa Janes
Marta Johnson
Michelle Johnson
Olga Johnson
Holly Jones
Susan Jones
Elaine Kamradt
Amy L. Keane
Virginia Kendrick
Ellen Kent
Jeff Kerr, Blue Water Grill
Vicki Keyser
Shirley Kiisk
Beth Kiisk-Milanowski
Melissa Klunejko
Antoinette Knapp
Lisa Martinez Kreager
Leigh Kubiak
Kuiper Family
Jennifer Laven
Karen Lawrence
Stacy Levitt
Pam Liggett
Sheryl Lilly
Jessica Lincolnhol
Marcia Love
Jennifer MacLaren
Peggy Magnesen
Diane Mangnuson
Melissa March

Pat Marks
David McClimans, Marigold Lodge
Jill McCormick
Michelle McDermott
Cathy McKenzie
Mary Beth Mead
Judy Mick
Tara Millar
Connie Miller
Kate Molumby
Kirsetin K. Morello
Tanya Muehlbauer
Christina Mustert
Margaret Nault
Cecily Near
Joanne Ajlouny Nicola
Kristine Nisper
Karen O'Donovan
Diane O'nions
Kathy Olson
Mary Otolski
Joseph Pagano,
    Raffaela's by Pagano's
Linda Page
Judy Palmer
Shelley Parente
Connie Petter
Gabrielle Pollack
Margaret Pyle
Steve Radtke
Karen Rahn
Karen Rambo
Betsy Redman
Beth Reid
Patty Rhodes
Kristen Ringler
Anne Risch
Tami Myers Ross
Kim Rossi
Betty Roth
Bonnie Roth
Gina Roth
Glynn Ann Ruggeri
Julie Rupp
Anne Saliers
Nancy Schaefer
Marianne Schlick
Katie Schneider
Mike Schoenbom,
    Egypt Valley Country Club
Lorna Schultz
Susie Sebastian
Peter and Joan Secchia,
    Villa Taverna, residence of
    the U.S. Ambassador to Italy

Kim Shammas
Leslie Shape
Jackie Shepard
Beth Skaggs
Nancy Skinner
Lori Skoog
Barbara L. Smith
Sharon Smith
Jenell Spindle
Kelly Stecco
Dana Stenstrom
Cynnie Swain
Karol Tiemersma
Melissa Timmer
Terrence Timmer
Cheryl Timyan
Michelle Toering
Stacy Trierweiler
Thea Underwood
Vandenberg Family
Gretchen Vanderboegh
Barbara VanDongen
Holly G. VanLeuven
Edith Vasu
Joan Vos, Tulip Time Festival, Inc.
Lisbeth Votruba
Rebecca Vredenberg and Family
Nancy Wanty
Pat Waring
Kathy Warren
Tom Webb, The B.O.B.
Linda Welch
Laura Wickholm
David Wiener
Rebecca Wierda
Paula Williams
Anne Williamson
Janet Wilson
Kris Wilson
Catherine Winick
Corrie Witherell
Susan Wittenbach
Jen Wittlinger
Julie Wolf
Sandy Zimmer
Kari Zubrickas

Special Thank Yous

Jerry and Chris Barber
Jaye Beeler, The Grand Rapids Press
Catherine Behrendt
Scott Bernecker
William Bernecker
Lisa Cargill

Katrina Cranmer
Amelia Donohoe
Joe Donohoe
Cade Elliott
Val Enghauser
Mayor Judy Frey
Ray Greene
Josef Huber, Amway Grand Plaza
Brett Hurley, Aquinas College
Martha Jackson
Colleen Janes
Larry Johnson
Janet Korn,
    Grand Rapids/Kent County
    Convention & Visitors Bureau
Jeff Liggett
Pam Liggett
Marcia Love
Nat Love
Kathy Mahacek
Cindy Marat-Larsen, Muskegon Area
    Chamber of Commerce
Peter McDaniel
Jason Moore
Suzanne Moore
Cecily Near
Benjamin Neumann
Joanne Nicola
Shelley Parente
Louis and Wallene Poteau
Bill Race
Kevin Race
Meaghan Race
Tom and Karen Rambo
Kathy Rambo-Wagner
Mitch Ranger
Hannah Rinkevicz
Mark Rinkevicz
Justin Rowe
Julie Rupp
Selig Farms, Shelby, MI
Kelly Stecco
Sheri Stetson-Compton,
    The Grand Rapids Press
Peter Stuursma
Thea Underwood
Marlyn Walton
Alex Ward
Chris Waring
Madeleine Wilson
Matthew Wilson
Judi Young, The Gilmore Collection

Grand Temptations

Delightful Diversions from the Great Lakes State

Order Form

Order Date _____

Number of Books _____   @ $24.95 per book $ _____ (subtotal)

(Michigan residents add 6% of subtotal) Sales Tax $ _____

($4.95 for first book; add $2.00 for each additional book) Shipping $ _____

TOTAL AMOUNT $ _____

Prices subject to change without notice

METHOD OF PAYMENT (Checks, VISA, and MasterCard accepted):

Credit Card # _____   Exp Date _____

(VISA or MasterCard ONLY)

Name as it appears on Card _____

Signature _____   OR Check # _____

Checks made payable to:
Junior League of Grand Rapids

SOLD TO:

Name _____   Telephone (____)_____

Street Address _____

City _____   State _____   Zip Code _____

Email _____

SHIP TO (if different than Sold To):

Name _____   Telephone (____)_____

Street Address (cannot ship to PO boxes) _____

City _____   State _____   Zip Code _____

Please Mail or Fax this form to:
Junior League of Grand Rapids, Michigan
25 Sheldon Blvd SE
Grand Rapids, MI 49503
(616) 242-8422 telephone
(616) 451-1936 fax

www.juniorleaguegr.com   Thank you for your order!   grandtemptations@iserv.net